TALES *of a* NOT SO TINY HOUSE

TALES of a NOT SO TINY HOUSE

Chloe Barcelou
Brandon Batchelder

FOREWORD BY
MARY RANDOLPH CARTER

RIZZOLI
NEW YORK

New York · Paris · London · Milan

CONTENTS

Foreword 8
Introduction 10

I
ADRIFT
14

II
ROMANTIC INSPIRATIONS
26

III
IN THE WINGS
56

IV
BEFITTING A PRINCESS
76

V
BECOMING A MAN
100

VI
THE KITCHEN OF TOMORROW
124

VII
THE OLD CAPTAIN'S VANITY
152

VIII
TALL TALES
174

IX
LA VIE EN ROUGE
202

X
THE SPIRIT OF CHRISTMAS
220

EPILOGUE
DOWN THE LINE
248

Resources 252
Acknowledgments 254

*When we built this peculiar house, we knew there would be kindred souls out there who would understand it. We recognize you from time to time by the gleam in your eye—people of all ages who keep, somewhere within, a part that will never grow old. **This book is for you.***

FOREWORD

MARY RANDOLPH CARTER

From an early age I sought out little, cozy places to hide away in and create imaginary homes and stories for myself and my large family of dolls. Maybe it was because I was the oldest of nine—seven girls and two boys—that I had that need from time to time to escape to my own world. It started on the third floor of a big brick house on a tree-lined avenue in Richmond, Virginia. Our family lived on the first floor, and up the stairs on the second and third floors lived my mother's family—her father, her two aunts, and one of her two older sisters. I'm not sure why I was allowed to have two bedrooms—one on the first floor with my siblings and one on the third floor near Big Nell, my great aunt, and Boots, my aunt. It was in that cozy room that I created a dollhouse out of a cupboard of shelves and spent endless hours moving my miniature doll furnishings around and making little rugs and curtains out of scraps of fabric from Big Nell's sewing basket. I was ten when a fire ended that first cozy refuge. When we moved to another big house, I had my own room next door to my two younger sisters, and down the hall was the door to the attic that would become the site of my next pretend home. There was only one little window in the attic; light shined through it and onto the wooden rafters

that defined the long, narrow space filled with trunks and boxes and things abandoned—books and ballgowns and three-legged chairs and an antique cradle in which some distant cousin was rocked to sleep. On the floor near that window, I set up my dollhouse, and once surrounded by this comforting clutter I felt I was home again.

When I was twelve, we moved from Richmond to live in River Barn, a wonderful old house near the Rappahannock River where we had summered for years. I found my getaway in a storage building at the back of the house and slept summer nights in the little room above it. Later, when we moved up the road to Muskettoe Pointe Farm, our seventeenth-century home directly facing the river, I slept in a little weathered shed in a tangle of honeysuckle and grapevine that brought to mind the story of *The Secret Garden*. It had been a refuge for children's play, a writer's words, a gardener's toil, a place a little out of the fray where time passed not with the clock but with the shadows of the day. My first apartment in New York City was a fifth-floor walk-up filled with comforting things—an old wooden rocking chair, a faded green blanket chest, patchwork quilts—and memories of my life with the family I had left behind in Virginia. Living there was a little like living in that first dollhouse I had created down the hall from Big Nell so long ago.

When I first read about Chloe and Brandon's life in their magical caravan, it reminded me of all these memories of my own lifelong quest for magical hideaways—real or imagined! What these two have formed with their personal creativity and hard work is a home that is a dream! Stepping through the doorway into their life through this book is a gift. Reading their heartfelt stories and viewing each detail of how they brought their vision to life through this treasured scrapbook of imagery inspires our own ideas of what a home could be. Maybe not exactly like the tiny jewel of a home they have created, but one that is filled with the personal stories and warmth of the way we wish to live with the things we love.

INTRODUCTION

I can remember the feeling I had the day my brothers and I built a fort in our playroom. It was only a ruin of sofa cushions on the floor covered in blankets, but I couldn't have been more exhilarated by the prospect of our spending the night inside. Sentenced instead to sleep in our beds, we never did, but I never stopped dreaming about it.

We have all known that feeling—that calling to stay—whether it came from building a soft fort of pillows on the floor or one of prickly branches in the woods. We might have felt it scaling the precarious ladder of a just-finished treehouse or unpacking musty old camping gear to set up a cozy new site. It is a feeling Chloe and I know well. We had it the first night we climbed into the loft bed of this, our shiphouse, some ten years ago, and we've experienced it nearly every night since. Like birds settling down for the night outside, we have the primal urge to build a shelter, a nest, and settle into it for safety.

Maybe you've seen the video of a pet beaver trying to dam up a bathtub with toys it gathered from around the house. Though initially I found it adorable and funny, it broke my heart when I realized the busy little creature would never succeed in turning that house into a pond.

I have noticed that we humans, too, seem to be living in a different world than the one that forged our instincts. This is not news to us, living in the twenty-first

century, accustomed as we are to constant change, but shocking when you consider how relatively unchanging our human existence was for such a very long time. But somewhere around the Industrial Revolution, our way of life altered fundamentally. We went from a world where we harvested creatively from nature to meet our needs to one where most of us are removed from that process. That process, however, may not yet be removed from us.

I offer the popularity of the tiny house movement as evidence. There are many profound and valid reasons to build tiny homes on wheels: low cost of living, freedom of travel, simplification, sustainability, and so on. The tiny house is surely a solution to myriad problems, but I suspect that if you were to get underneath it all, more times than not you'd find people yearning to experience the natural pleasure of carving out little homes for themselves.

Not only is building a home prohibitively expensive, but a house's construction and installation also seem to require increasingly specialized design and knowledge. I adore the twenty-first century—in spite of the challenges we face, we've been given so much, and the view from atop our cultural, technological hill avails us a broader look through time than ever before—but I cannot help but notice that some of our progress has come at a cost, and I think we ought to know what it is.

When Chloe and I first sat down to write this book, we naturally considered writing a DIY manual, but after a great deal of thought, we realized that our creation is a byproduct of our specific story, the knowledge we possessed, and the resources to which we had access. Every person's situation will be different. There remains, however, an empowering truth to convey, which is that all of us, like the beaver, share something in common: we descend from wildly creative people, whose instincts, when fostered, are to transform the materials of our environment into our dreams.

OPPOSITE: Our tiny house parked at its third location: an apple orchard in New Hampshire. This picturesque spot is our favorite, so far.

I

ADRIFT

When Chloe and I first adopted our rabbit, Cosmos—known informally as Mr. Nose—we lived in a little carriage house on an old woodland farm in New Hampshire. Inside, the walls were drafty enough to blow out a candle, and parts of the exposed timbers had been smoothed to a shine by the touch of human hands over the course of centuries. When you ran your own hands over that glossy surface, you could feel the history. You could feel yourself becoming a part of it.

We loved it there. It was our first place together. Outside, free-range chickens roamed the property like little marauding dinosaurs, while the farm's two horses whinnied from over the fence whenever we came into view, and the thousands of acres that surrounded the farm were wild and beautiful, especially in the early spring, when the newly thawed forest and pastures were so brilliantly green. My father would occasionally visit, every time falling asleep as he sat by the woodstove muttering, "Good ole wood heat." He told me that the time I lived there might just turn out to be the best time of my life.

Of course, my father knew there was more to our life together than sunshine and sweetness. The cabin was cheap enough for Chloe and me to rent because it wasn't near anything, and despite the fact that we seemed always to be working, we struggled to make ends meet.

This was our first place together, a charming one-room cabin with a frame made of salvaged timbers.

A cozy evening after dinner. The fridge was free off Craigslist. We eventually painted it with chalkboard paint.

Built from the remains of an old torn-down Shaker house, this dusty little cottage won us over with its charm the moment we opened the door.

The stairs led to a small, sloped-ceiling loft. We brought Cosmos up one night, but his sprinting and jumping on our faces while we attempted to sleep dissuaded us from proffering a second invitation.

We loved the cozy atmosphere the sturdy beams created, and how we could utilize them to display baskets and hang lights, lanterns, and hammocks. We were inspired by their functionality and aesthetic, so much so that we later incorporated faux beams into our own tiny home design.

We hung string lights across the beams of our kitchen and used a camp stove to cook.

Starting the day feeding these majestic animals is a meditation we sorely miss. Someday . . .

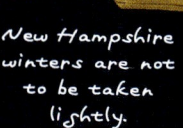

New Hampshire winters are not to be taken lightly.

Contemplating life while overlooking the horse pastures at sunset.

Country living agreeing with Brandon.

Our first rabbit, Cosmos.

Dressing up every day is essential for Chloe's well-being.

Shelves stacked with books overseen by librarian Cosmos, aka Mr. Nose, Conosemister, Mipper Nove, Mipperskapernova, Mip, Skap, and Skack.

We had also moved into the carriage house at the onset of winter, which is, of course, not a season to take lightly in New Hampshire. One of the things we loved about the place was the little woodstove. I had grown up by one, and all the toiling that goes along with heating a house with wood was something I very much enjoyed, but the sobering cold of early winter, along with the bleak realization that we didn't have enough money to buy proper cordwood, sent us on a wild goose chase for anything that we could burn. Eventually, I bought a pile of green pine in desperation, and I spent the rest of the winter with my head in the stove, struggling to keep the wet wood burning and the drafty house from freezing.

We were at something of a crossroads then. Inevitable, big life changes quietly loomed as we walked old paths that no longer seemed on course. For my part, I had known I wanted to be a carpenter from the time I could stand, but by the time I was old enough to make my own way in the world, I had realized that the reality of the trade was not what I had naively imagined it to be—kindly old men, wearing suspenders, spectacles, and marvelous beards, crafting woodwork like fine art as they spouted folksy wisdom. Instead, I found myself working for surly construction crews that threw together dozens of bloated, characterless houses at a time, leveling swaths of wilderness along the way. It was not for me.

What was for me was something I would struggle to sort out. I would try my hand at many disparate paths over the years. I studied and taught martial arts, I worked in special education, I worked as a welder, I worked for an electrician, I moved furniture, I went to college, I built and test-rode Segways, and the list goes on.

Chloe, meanwhile, had been struggling to sort out her own story. Her whole life, she had loved photography, and the painted portraiture that preceded its invention. She had been deeply inspired by artists from Frida Kahlo to Tim Walker, who crafted sets, props, and wardrobes, posing elegant models in thematic roles, and she loved to put together her own shoots. Now, in the undisturbed quiet of rural New England, she saw an opportunity to dig into her craft.

The winter leading up to Chloe's bright idea, however, was a long one, and night after night we found ourselves worn down by the bitingly cold wind that swept up the valley, rattling the windows and whistling through the cracks in the old timbers. Heating with only a woodstove meant getting up in the middle of the night to tend the fire, and more than once the drip in the kitchen sink became an icicle. It was charming, in a Charles Dickens–meets–Laura Ingalls Wilder sort of way, but my fifteen-hour workdays were catching up with me. I was at that point in a small business venture—I had been trying to bridge the transition from teaching martial arts privately to running my own brick-and-mortar studio—where all it takes is one more logistical straw on the camel's back to make you ask yourself, do I really want this *this* badly? I decided it was time to let go of the night work for a while, and convalesce with my girl until my mind was again well enough to form its own bright ideas.

Bittersweet though it was, we were soon consoled by the growing warmth and lengthening days of springtime, and Chloe and I reveled in my newfound ability to make it home in time for leisurely sunset walks in the forest. Chloe enjoyed the benefit of my being around to lend a hand on her shoots, and though we made even less money, we had discovered that the town recycling center had a glorious invention known as the swap shed. This was a place where people could discard the things they didn't want, but that were too nice to throw away. Our dump day ritual was born. Every Saturday, we would splurge on a cup of coffee from the general store and venture out in search of treasure. It was hit-or-miss, but we were thrilled on occasion to find old steamer trunks, trinkets, furniture, and all manner of curiosities. Over time, and with the help of the odd yard sale find, our little cabin, like the world outside, began to blossom.

To boot, we now had a shy rescue bunny, a sweet little thing who fell in love with my slippers first, then my feet, then me. He was gracious enough to court me in traditional rabbit fashion: grooming my bare skin, which is the gentle bunny nibbling that declares, you belong to me.

Things were looking up. Chloe's work in photography was progressing, and people and publications were beginning to take notice. Eventually, a first-time filmmaker saw her work and thought she would make a great production designer for his debut film (but as is often the case with film work, nothing came of that for another year).

Though my craftsman skills had become mostly dusty, Chloe began to put them to use on her shoots, and the marriage of our combined aptitudes, which were natural and complementary, gradually began to reveal a new future of possibilities.

In many ways, my father was right: it was the best time of my life. But just as in a fairy tale, we had our share of dragons to contend with, and when one of them reared its head, we found it necessary to pack up our things and move.

Chloe and a team of creatives on the set of her Steampunk Couture photo shoot in 2013.

Dedication (as written by Brandon in 2013 on the back of the artwork)

Here is some five months' measure of work, which, for pardon of grief-laden faculties, was long in the conjuring. For, in the time before this piece, there lived a man, my father, who in spirit of completion and pride passed on the tenth early morning of April 2013. In life, the warmth and humor of his good nature shone so vivid a message of love, loyalty, and well-wishing assurance that even from the boundless chasm of death it did brim and overflow and wash our hearts of a horror that had no place. And, when in a clearing of conscience, we beheld he had one more gift to bestow, a great blessing of firm understanding: His was the honor of going in ease so that we may yield him thus. And so, my good father, good man, and good friend did with the steadfast and tranquil ease of a seagoing vessel move to and from life remorseless, intrepid, and true. And yet, sure though I was of his will, the bigger part of my cheer did stir and draw after in the wake of that gentle passing. And so, this, "Antithesis," I undertook, so named after the music and color of light and life to which I had, in heartache, become blind, and in imagining did reclaim, for the sake of my beloved father, Robert Louis Batchelder Jr. 1942-2013

Bartering with our landlord, we worked off a month's rent by retiling the shower in our bungalow. We were thankful to learn how to cut and install stone tiles properly, expanding our skills.

Opposite: When I worked in elementary education, I enjoyed drawing on the chalkboards at lunch—and loved how easy it was to correct mistakes. This is the only pastel I haven't erased. I worked on it cathartically for four months, but not knowing how to seal it, I used a bad combination of sealants and watched the drawings dissolve before my eyes. I started over that day, and finished in another month. —B

Making a custom piece of set dressing—a privacy screen—for Chloe's Marie Antoinette fantasy photoshoot.

You can make your own chalkboard paint by mixing any color of flat paint with unsanded tile grout. The grout gives the paint the gritty texture necessary for the chalk to adhere to the surface.

However, the move wasn't all bad news. A chance encounter at a how-to-market-your-art seminar introduced us to an intriguing gentleman who lived in our town. Delightfully eccentric, he was an artist who applied his talent to stonework and old-world carpentry. Now seventy, he had begun building his home on a hill (verging on a mountain) forty years prior, and never stopped adding on. Everywhere, there were wonderful works of architecture—each nearly finished—and among the aesthetic sprawl, there was a charming bungalow waiting for someone to occupy it.

To my delight, there were workshops and tools of every kind on the premises. I was thrilled at the notion of getting to know the trades again, in the way that I had as a boy—wooden mallets, chisels, block-planes, and all.

The bungalow was a tightly packed collection of playful craftsmanship, and it was another place that was heated only by a woodstove. I was consoled by the fact that I could continue living by fire. In the bedroom, there was a high-seated bed with bare trees for posts, like Max's in *Where the Wild Things Are*. We could nestle in and look out the great rear window to a sunset stretching over rolling New Hampshire hillsides for twenty miles. We were surrounded by charm and humor. Had my father not suddenly passed away the very day we moved in, I can only imagine how happy Chloe and I might have been.

It's hard to measure the loss of a man like my dad. In some families, a single person plays more than a single part. Their faith and pride in the ones they love draws in people like the pull of a great celestial body, spinning together in orbit people who might otherwise drift away from one another. When you lose such a person, you can lose the others—and your very identity, if you're not careful. Such was the feeling that I had in those days. My father had been my best friend and my regular companion, and in my grief, I went a little mad.

On the little mountain, life did carry on. Though Chloe shouldered the burden of my grief, she somehow still managed to make strides in her career. I, on the other hand, found it difficult to put myself back together. To my great fortune, however, my father had been a consistent man in life, and by the time of his unexpected death,

I knew in my bones that he wanted me to live well. So, I cried until I couldn't cry anymore, and then I poured my grief into a commemorating art piece—chalk pastels on a chalkboard, a habit I picked up working in elementary schools—transmuting my pain into something beautiful. And I went about living all the more, as though a piece of his soul had gotten into mine and made it larger.

Then some extraordinary news came our way. That film producer called back, the movie was on, and Chloe was to be its production designer. The only problem was that they didn't have a set-builder. As luck would have it, Chloe knew a guy.

Soon, we would depart the bungalow on the hill, which we always understood was only temporary, the craftsman would find another traveler to fill our vacancy, and we would trade our one-store town for Boston. But the question we had in our minds was, where would we live after the film was over? Fortuitously, a trend that was at first a ripple was growing into a swell: tiny houses. On wheels.

I remember Chloe bustling down the stairs into my and the rabbit's chalk pastel dust cloud like it was only yesterday. "You might think I'm crazy," she said, "but I have an idea." As I listened to her proposal, the boy living in me perked up and paid attention, as though he—the one who built tree forts, go-carts, and zip lines as a child—had been waiting for a say for twenty years, and after all this time was being called upon to speak up, and in a big way.

As she pitched, I listened silently, and the idea of a tiny house on wheels clicked through every chink of consideration in my mind like a master key, solving problem after problem. We could live anywhere. We could look for work anywhere, and we would never have to leave a beloved home behind again. We could design and build it ourselves, without anyone telling us what to do. It was perfect, and as Chloe went on, questioning herself all the while, unsure whether I would think the idea was crazy, I listened with a glowing heart. If the rabbit didn't approve, he said nothing. For me, there was no decision. The only possible reply was a simple, heartfelt yes. We'd do the film, and then we'd build our tiny home. We might still find ourselves adrift in this world, but at least we'd have a ship.

❦ II ❦
ROMANTIC INSPIRATIONS

Thinking back to 2014, when my ideas for our little home were not yet more than a collection of influences circling in my mind, I am reminded of the first of many wishes Chloe would make for its design: a Tudor-style cottage. It is hard to imagine that this ship-like contraption in which we have so long now lived was once intended to be a simple, narrow house with white plaster panels and a fiercely pitched, high-reaching roof.

It has long been a belief of mine that things design themselves, once you've answered the first and most difficult question: Where do I begin? But now that I think of it, I cannot recollect having such a belief until this house made me understand it to be true. Decision by decision, I gradually began to feel we were more *discovering* its design than *inventing* it. Indeed, the complex structure in which we now live seems to have become inevitable from the first moment we knew a single, certain thing about it.

Though the steep sloping roof of a Tudor cottage was a feature that would ultimately prove too poor a use of space, choosing an alternative shape would mark the first tip in a long line of domino-like decisions. A steeply pitched roof would shed rain and snow nicely, but the trade-off would be less living space within. A flat roof offered the most room inside, but the rain and snow would harmfully linger. A compromise was all that remained, and it availed itself in the form of a gently rounded roof, a pretty line that instantly brought to mind an image of a dusty old steamer trunk, wrapped in buckles and filigreed hardware, top bulging, a curve further flattered by inward-canted sides. It's the kind of thing that promises mystery in an old person's attic.

The elegant shape was engineering perfection, and it brought to mind something we had seen many times before, especially in great classic movies, like *The Wolfman* (the remake of which, starring Benicio del Toro, Chloe and I had watched together on one of our first dates). It resembled the iconic caravan of the Romani people, the original wheeled tiny house builders, whose constant traveling has been a veritable emblem of freedom and romance for the ages, a shape perfected over time.

The first domino had been struck; we needed only to follow the tumbling. Romantic old steamer trunks also made us think of romantic old train cars, and the canted-in walls of the caravan combined with our Tudor cottage framing immediately brought to mind romantic old ships. Indeed, if there was a design inspiration that was *romantic* and *old*, it was tickling our fancy. There was only one fancy left to factor in, and as I looked at her, smiling with eyes that sparkled in anticipation of all the lovely things she could find to bejewel our future cottage, I knew one thing for certain: I would have to design for her the biggest tiny house I could imagine.

OPPOSITE: My work apron has saved many of my fancier garments from being demoted to painting clothes. I've worn it on all manner of projects, from films to messy tiny-home jobs. Each color paints a memory. —C

There is a wonderful term we have heard woodworkers use to describe the process of inserting the uncooperative spindles of a rocking chair into their respective holes. They cannot go in one at a time; they must be "worried" into place all at once.

<u>Hideously Smitten Couple Needs Temporary Build Site for
Charming, Innovative Tiny Home Contraption</u>

You Can't Get There from Here

We may be foolish for choosing the careers we have—Chloe chases styling gigs for magazine shoots and films, and I build what she needs for props and sets while troubling myself on the side writing and illustrating. Our lives were simpler to explain when I had a day job paying just enough to feed us, shelter us, and pay for the car that brought me to and from work. But it was a cycle, a trap, and we wanted out, and not because we didn't want to work like some people may think, but because we wanted our work to matter more, and the difficult truth was that meaningful work didn't often pay so well. So when Chloe came to me one day and said we should build a tiny home on wheels, because it was a cheaper way to live, because it would give us the freedom to travel and take jobs wherever they were, and that it would be a home we could fall in love with freely, never fearing that day when we would pack up that last box and say goodbye, I agreed. Just agreed; like Spock when the logic was "undeniable."

This past year we were fortunate to land our first big movie gig (big for us, mind you). I built the set, and Chloe styled it and made the costumes (Check it out if you'd like. It's called <u>Aimy in a Cage</u>. It's not released yet, but you can Google it.) It was a wonderful experience, and we are encouraged to seek more work like it. The best part is that we were able to strip the materials and stockpile them for our tiny home, some seven hundred two-by-fours! Free!

I set to work two months ago designing our tiny home, and it was no simple task. We both needed work spaces, clothing storage—Chloe has "a bit" more clothing than I—not to mention appropriate kitchen, sleeping, lounging, we are not exceptional in that regard. However, when you see that our roof and walls expand when we are parked, that it is designed after the feel of an old ship, a railroad car, a steamer trunk, and <u>Howl's Moving Castle</u>, you'll know that this work was not intended to follow the tiny home movement; it is intended to contribute.

What we need now is space to build, with access to electricity. I am projecting two and a half to four months building time. We wish to finish and haul before winter, basically, but the sooner the better. After all, we're breaking some new ground, and it is better to be ahead of schedule than behind. We are willing to pay for space, but our funds are rapidly dwindling, so we're hoping for somebody gentle. We are also willing to work out trade arrangements, too, like landscaping in exchange, etc.

I can promise you that we are polite, respectful, friendly, and appropriate, but, if I were you, I'd want more than my simple assurance, so of course we are prepared to offer as many character references as needed to answer any questions you have and alleviate any concerns.

I hope this posting finds you well, whether you are in a position to help us or not, but, if our adventure is something you are interested in discussing, please contact me via my email. Perhaps we can meet and talk things over via some good coffee, our treat.

　　　Yours Truly,
　　　Brandon Louis Batchelder

The Craigslist ad we ran when seeking land on which to build.

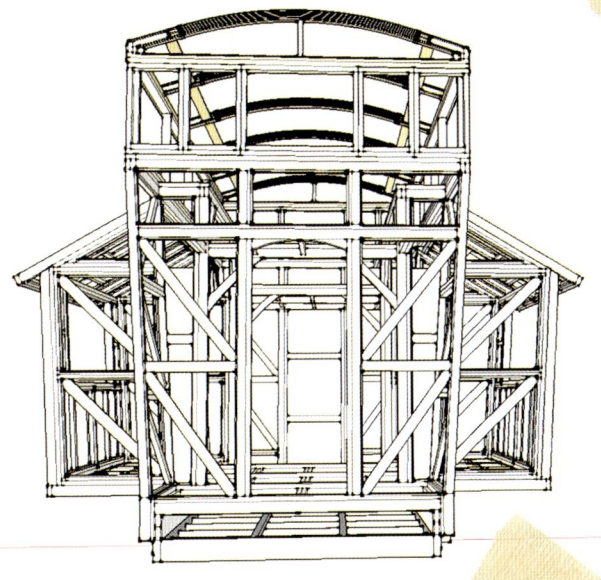

These are SketchUp renderings of our design. I raised the floor so that the folding sections can go over the wheel wells. This created what we call "the conspicuous cavity." One day it will harbor a retractable deck. —B

I found SketchUp to be a powerful tool for designing precise dimensions. The little man included in the program is helpful for setting a sense of scale. I eventually replaced him with an image of Jeff Bridges from The Big Lebowski, for better atmosphere. —B

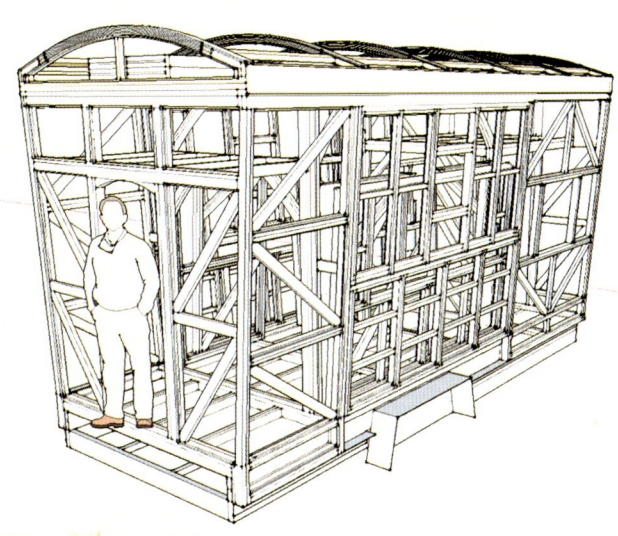

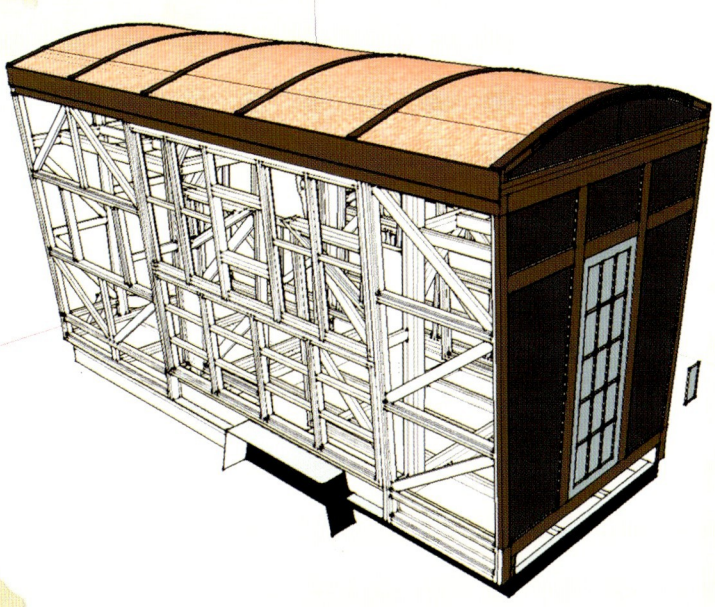

There is very little room inside our house when it is collapsed, especially now that our folding walls are hung with built-in storage. Interior design for us is twofold—we have to think about not only where things will look good when the house is expanded, but also where they will fit when the house is collapsed. —B

Construction

Finding a place to build our house would prove more challenging than we imagined. First, I spent a month hunting down a used utility trailer on Craigslist that would serve as the foundation for our house. While searching, I was able to make use of the time by editing my nebulous design. Believe it or not, I had been prepared just to arrive somewhere with a pile of wood and wing it. I'm always curious about how that house might've come out.

My design process started off with a lot of sitting around, talking with Chloe, thinking, and sketching, but eventually I needed to find a more dynamic medium to work out the moving parts of our coalescing vision. I bought a piece of rigid foam and sliced it up into scaled down "timbers," which I then pinned together with broken toothpicks. This worked out excellently, and once it was completed, Google's SketchUp—a design program I would painstakingly learn to use by working out the inch-by-inch minutiae of our complicated structure—became an invaluable tool.

Around this time Chloe spotted an HGTV casting call for the new show Tiny House, Big Living. Chloe applied, HGTV took the bait, and after a Skype call the producers appeared to be interested, but I wonder if they weren't a little skeptical of my ambitious plan. It sounded naive, like something a child would imagine: "We'll be using a ship's wheel and pulleys to hoist the roof!" Whether for that or other reasons, they would keep our names, but pass us over for their pilot episode.

Finally, I found a trailer for one thousand dollars, and we were ready to begin, or so we thought. We were living in Boston at the time. A friend had lent us their vacant house in exchange for our renovating it to sell, but it had no room for a sprawling build outside, so after exhausting the short list of people we knew, the quest was on for some trusting soul who would let perfect strangers build a house, on a trailer, in their yard. What could go wrong?

After we posted an ad on Craigslist, about thirty people responded. Some sounded crazy, others scary. A few were intrigued, but only two were cautiously open to the idea.

The first couple we met were very nice. They offered their land for us to build on for a mere two hundred dollars a month and promptly disappeared, and we were unable to reach them again. Fortuitously, however, the last person I spoke with was a calm, soft-spoken gentleman I liked immediately. I had become so accustomed to people turning bizarre at some point in the conversation that I was bracing for the man eventually to reveal a mean streak, but as we talked, he simply asked me one matter of fact question after another: "Do you need electricity? How much space do you need?"

He was an electrical engineer, about the age my dad would have been. He was living quietly in Hampton, New Hampshire, along with his effervescent wife, a retired special education teacher.

They immediately reminded us of the couple in Pixar's Up. Where he was tranquil and reserved, she was exuberant and warm, and it wasn't long before we were moving our things into the little green clearing in their backyard. And best yet, they didn't want anything in return but for us to succeed.

I had the timber ready to go. The right way to build a film set is to make flats, sections of wall made of sheets of very thin plywood that set builders attach to light, wooden frames. Efficient and arrangeable, these flats can be affixed together and configured to make rooms of just about any shape. They are the building blocks of set design, but we didn't learn about them until after I finished building our first feature-film set, which I built like a house, with two-by-fours and tons of Sheetrock.

After the film was completed, the Sheetrock, tragically, was unsalvageable, but we rescued the pile of some seven hundred two-by-fours from the dumpster to build the frame of our home. The only problem was that these modern studs weren't what we wanted them to be: chunky old timbers with character. We would solve this problem by cutting off their round edges, and gluing and screwing the smaller studs together to make bigger beams of varying dimensions, after which I would "age" them by shaving diagonal cuts to mimic the evidence of an old hewing axe.

So, while Chloe picked up the odd commercial gig to keep us fed, I began building in a frenzy in September, when the weather was heavenly. It was a golden time. Chloe came to help whenever she could, but it didn't take long for us to realize that our two-and-a-half-month estimate was preposterous, and within a few months, we found ourselves building in the infamous New England winter of 2014 to 2015. Still, by the tail end of the winter's barrage of snowstorms, we had managed to get the frame up, just in time for HGTV to call us back.

Mostly off camera, we set to working harder than ever, striving at least to present the appearance of a completed structure for the show's spring deadline. Some viewers would later notice that we didn't have plumbing, but most didn't notice that we also didn't have a front doorknob, or a staircase to reach it.

We worked until June, as many as eighteen hours a day by the end, and when the cameras arrived, we fumbled through questions with foggy brains, but elated spirits.

In the end, it took a village. Friends we hadn't seen in years found time to drop in and lend a hand, and together we raised the house like the proverbial barn. The only catch was, those folks in the old days really knew what they were doing. In just a few years, mother nature would teach us where we had gone wrong.—B

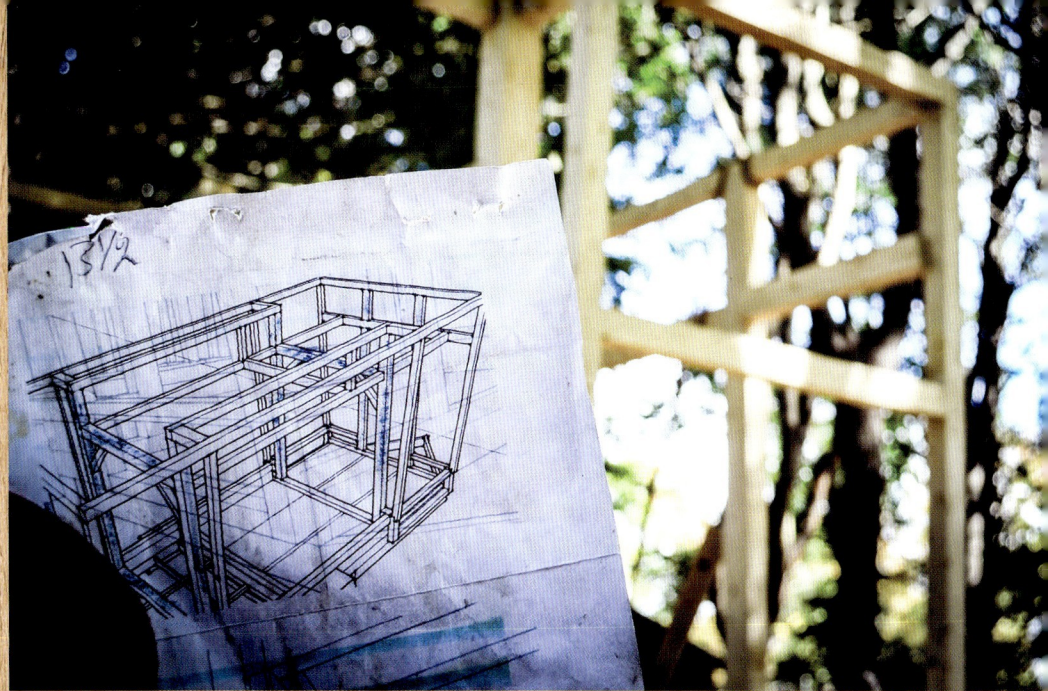

CLOCKWISE FROM TOP LEFT:
Once the structure was up and covered, it became our workshop—we could finally work in the rain! The blueprint—the trailer had different measurements than we had expected, so we adjusted to fit. We created the roof arches by laminating, gluing, and screwing strips of thin plywood over a mold. Timber-frame inspired, the plywood paneling we installed next further strengthened the structure. This is the trailer our house is built upon. We relegated its wooden side rails to the burn pile, until we later ran out of wood. When we scratched the fence's surface, we were surprised to see that it looked like mahogany. We have since repurposed it to make our countertop, ladder, toolbox, and a swing.

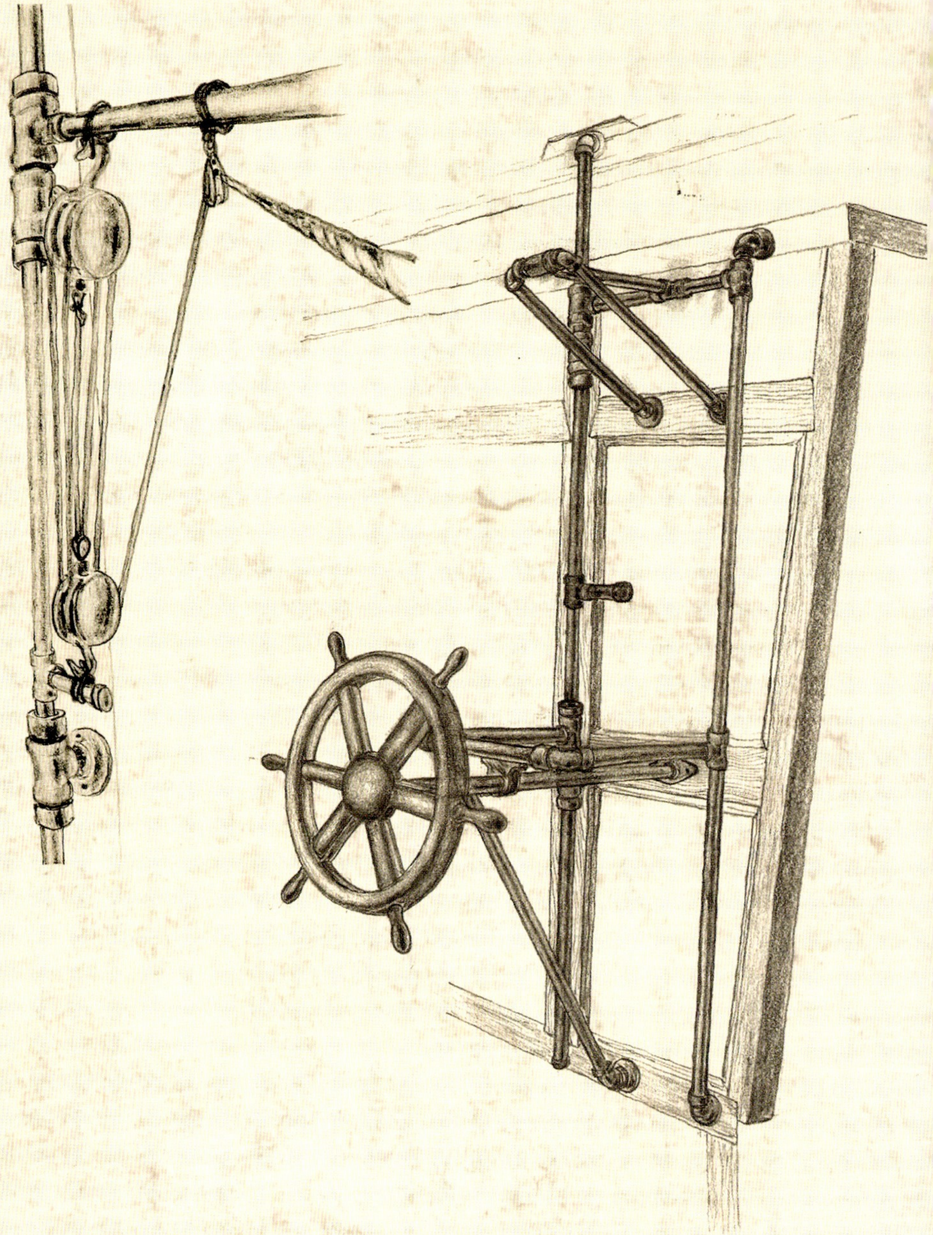

ABOVE: *Brandon's original sketch for the roof hoist.*

TOP LEFT: *I am always impressed by Brandon's inventions, so when he had the idea to raise the roof to create more space/combat my sleeping loft–induced claustrophobia, I trusted him (although I never fully understood the physics that he explained, re-explained, and even demonstrated to me). Later, those pesky HGTV producers got into my ear and my head, asking, "What if the roof hoist mechanism doesn't work?" To my relief, the roof hoisted as planned, as demonstrated for the first time during the filming of our episode, but I laugh, as I think to myself, "But what if it didn't work?" I hadn't even considered it.* —C

CENTER LEFT: *The ship's wheel drives the spool, the spool pulls four ropes that go to block and tackle pulleys, and the pulleys draw the legs of the roof upward.*

BOTTOM LEFT: *Brandon's friend Scott came with his pipe bender, and together they fabricated the spool.*

OPPOSITE: *Our original paint job that didn't last.*

Several years in, high humidity inside the first iteration of the tiny house made renovation necessary. The moisture pushed through the walls and bubbled the paint on the exterior panels and roof. This disaster could have been avoided simply by cracking some windows!

We took the opportunity to reinforce the roof with steam-bent arches. Brandon used a garment steamer and duct pipe to do this. We gutted the rot around the house, painted inside the walls, reinsulated with closed cell foam that can't absorb water, and covered the roof with aluminum sheeting.

1. Bending plank to fit mold.

2. Duct pipe steam chamber.

3. Installing new trim and paneling.

4. We called rot removal "rooting out the evil."

5. Staining with timber oil while the bent wood set.

1. Exposed side paneling drying out.
2. Some very sketchy roof scaffolding.
3. A look at our waterproof rigid-foam insulation.
4. Subarch for attaching aluminum sheets.
5. Additional reflective insulation on roof.
6. Yay, aluminum! Unpleasant temporary plastic office walls, nay.

If you're living in a small space, consider an air exchanger. It expels air from inside, while drawing in fresh air. The heat from the outgoing air is transferred to the incoming air, so you don't lose warmth. It's an excellent way to keep a small space from becoming too humid.

At the height of our humidity problems, it was so moist, we didn't have to water our Christmas tree at all.

I dreamed of owning this very ornate lantern even before I met Brandon, having seen it in an antique store years before. The seller told me that it was brought to him by a couple of witches from Salem, Massachusetts. The alleged witches had procured it from someone in New Orleans, where presumably the light had hung in a mysterious location for many decades. — C

LEFT: The original lauan plywood paneling we salvaged from a film set, painted gunmetal gray, beginning to show signs of moisture, circa 2017. RIGHT: Our new black recycled-plastic paneling with orange peel texture. We wanted to find something salvaged to replace our rotting paneling. After searching everywhere for ideas, we found a company that uses mixed recycled plastic (industrial and consumer) for its plastic lumber products. This marine grade, UV-stabilized material will outlast us and requires no maintenance.

Seeing the shadow our door cast on this spooky pumpkin made us dream of lamps that cast tree shadows so we can take the forest with us, even if we're parked in urban locations.

We found our front door at a flea market. We arrived late morning, and the vendors were already packing up when I spotted the door. It looked like it had come straight off of a pirate's ship! I deduced that it had most likely been used in a restaurant. I asked the vendor how much, almost wincing as I did because I knew the cost of doors. "Twenty-five dollars!" he exclaimed. I hesitated for a moment in disbelief, scanning the crowd for Brandon. "Okay, twenty dollars!" said the vendor. Maybe if I had kept waiting, I could have gotten it for ten! — C

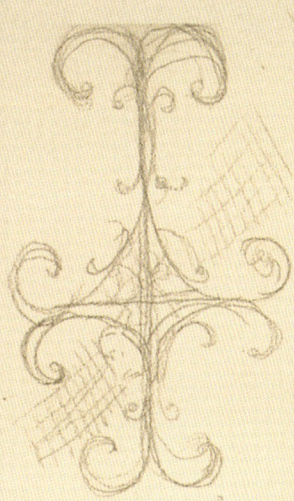

Tediously scraping off layers of paint with a heat gun.

The original base coat we mistakenly applied (over the existing varnish, no less).

We've learned the difference between painting with regular paint and using a penetrating oil. For exterior projects that endure a lot of sunshine and harsh New England winters—which cause a lot of expansion and contraction—we prefer a penetrating stain like a timber oil. Even our preferred linseed oil-based paint is penetrating, ensuring we never have to waste time scraping off old product; we can simply add an additional coat when wear begins to show.

Applying a coat of penetrating oil with a wash technique.

Fitting our five-dollar thrifted brass knocker.

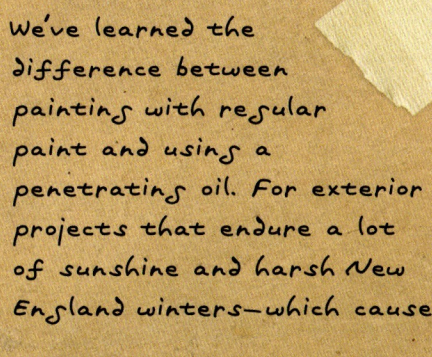

Contemplating the fit of the door and the custom corner brackets to be made and installed.

Painting gold leaf details on the door.

I have always loved Chloe's scrolly doodles, so I asked her to sketch some for our screen door. —B

Freehanding our silhouettes, using a photo for reference.

Using a plasma cutter from the local makerspace to cut out the design.

Two themes recurred throughout my iterations of the screen door design: roses and spiderwebs. I'm sure I was subconsciously inspired by Beauty and the Beast. Brandon and I incorporated them into the final design. —C

Cutting out the template.

Chloe's sketch for incorporating our initials into the bottom of the screen door.

The art of the silhouette—contrast and juxtaposition—has always fascinated me. When I was a child, my mother hired artists to create silhouette portraits of myself and my siblings. Immortalized in our metal door, Brandon and I will now always be here to greet our guests.—C

THE GREAT FLAPPY HOUSE INCIDENT OF 2015

"The sea was angry that day, my friends." —GEORGE COSTANZA

At the exit of New England's infamously challenging winter of 2014 and 2015, a weather event descended onto our build, leaving behind a cautionary tale with which we still regale our friends.

We had recently upgraded our derelict camp of small, mixed tarps to one sheltered by a glorious, monochromatic sail of polyethylene—a 60-foot giant that when filled with the warmth of our kerosene heater seemed to swell and float in the calm of New England's "fool's spring."

It became so warm inside the dome of pleasantness that Chloe and I and our friends Jason and Jacob, who kindly came to help for a few days, took off our coats and worked comfortably in T-shirts. Had I been a wiser man, I might have considered that the day's calm was, in fact, a little too calm.

We heard it first in the rattling of the bare tree branches across the field. Seconds later, a frigid blast of seaside wind hit us like a rogue wave, pelting us with stinging hail and tugging so hard at our parachute of a tarp that I thought the house might go.

Jacob and I ran to secure the tarp's ends and held fast, but we morons were no match for the tsunami of wind that ripped the tarp from our hands like we weren't there, and flicked it aside to wrap around some indignant trees.

For a while, we scrambled around like Forrest Gump when the hurricane hit his shrimpin' boat, uncertain what to do, and then we got to wrestling the tarp like a team of people carrying an enormous, angry snake. At one point, the snake snagged under our work bench, and Jason, struggling to lift it let out a cry like the Highlander after he defeats a foe, and all that lightning power comes into to him. Another yawp later, and he managed to heft the bench and loose the tarp.

After a half hour's battling, the tarp was again protecting our vulnerable build, but the wind—in like a lion—blew for a week straight. We couldn't rest for a moment without that tarp starting to weasel loose from here or there, before we would grab it, clamp it, tie it, something. And the flapping—the constant flapping. It wore on our nerves. If you were working near the side of the house, it would flap at you or catch you off guard with a flap against your head or back. We became unhinged. We started to call it the flappy house, and in our delirium, we thought that sounded like the title of an Adam Sandler movie, and we went around saying Adam Sandler-y things in our best Sandler voices: "Why you so flappy-flappy!" or "Hey! You kids wanna see the flappy house?" To this day, we wonder what the neighbors must have thought.

The moral, my good mates, is to mind your tarps wisely. Leave no gap through which the gnawing wind might enter. And trust ye never a fool's spring.

Growing up, I loved to read, and one of my favorite series was The Boxcar Children, *mysteries about a group of siblings who escape home to live in a train car. Either I read this collection at an impressionable age, or the idea of caravan-living was always in my heart.—C*

III
IN the WINGS

In a cruel irony, every adult seems to desire desperately the one thing children loathe above all: sleep. Commands to put on my pajamas and brush my teeth sent shivers down my spine that I can still feel. But ever since the invention of sending children to bed, there has been a silver lining: the bedtime story. I didn't always get one, but when I did, it was the best part of the night.

When I was a child, my father used to read to me a book called *The Flying Hockey Stick*. It was the whimsical story of a boy who wanted to see the world, so, naturally, he used household items, like a fan, an umbrella, a hockey stick, and all the extension cords he could get his hands on, to construct a flying machine. The lad used his invention to fly around the world rescuing new friends from various perilous situations just in the nick of time, until he ran out of extension cord and sandwiches and had to turn back.

As I think back on this absurd and lovely tale—and my childhood selves still inside me like the inner rings of an aging tree, enjoying the funny story and my father's company—I cannot help but notice how stories like this one have influenced Chloe and me. We have, in a sense, built our own absurd flying machine. Our home really began to look, at least to a child's eye, like something that could fly once we built the wings—as we have come to call the folding side sections that make up our respective *his and hers* quarters.

Over the course of our lives, many stories have continued to inspire us. Not all of them were books, of course. There are the countless films we have come to cherish: Pixar's *Up*, *Howl's Moving Castle*, *Hook*. There are so many more, all wild flying tales of fantasy. As we look around this absurd and whimsical flying ship of our own, we can see the spirit of these stories warmly reflected. We may have decided to build a traveling house because we needed one, but if you look deeper, you'll see that we also built it because we needed to make room for something else in our lives.

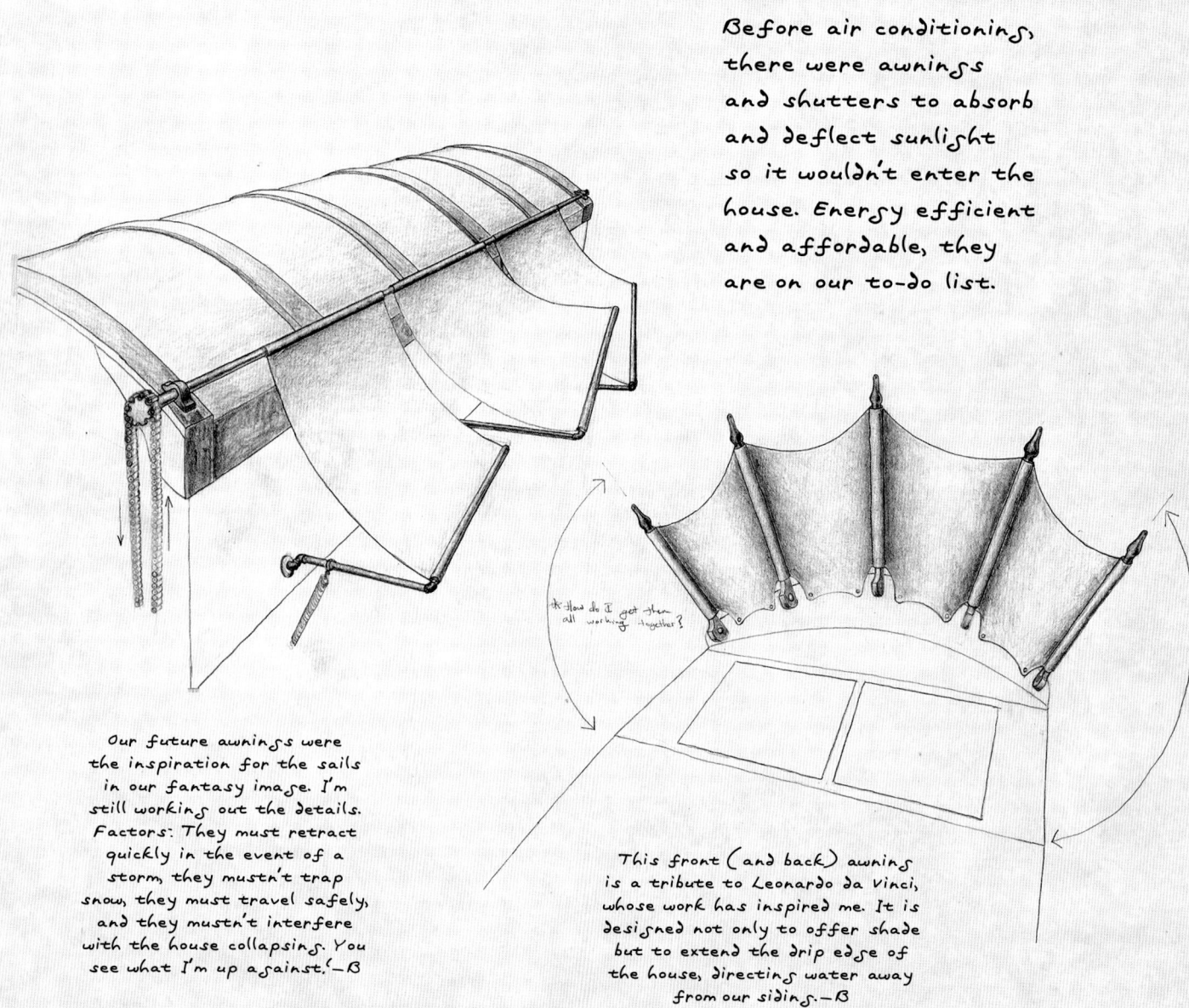

Before air conditioning, there were awnings and shutters to absorb and deflect sunlight so it wouldn't enter the house. Energy efficient and affordable, they are on our to-do list.

Our future awnings were the inspiration for the sails in our fantasy image. I'm still working out the details. Factors: They must retract quickly in the event of a storm, they mustn't trap snow, they must travel safely, and they mustn't interfere with the house collapsing. You see what I'm up against. —B

This front (and back) awning is a tribute to Leonardo da Vinci, whose work has inspired me. It is designed not only to offer shade but to extend the drip edge of the house, directing water away from our siding. —B

In the Wings

1.

2.

3.

Built to accommodate road restrictions for height and width, our house measures 13 feet tall and 8½ feet wide when collapsed. When expanded, it gains 2 feet, 8 inches in height, and the wings grow to 14 feet wide. Items that aren't built in must be packed up when we move, which isn't often, as is evidenced here by our expanding the house in the wrong order. The sides should open first!

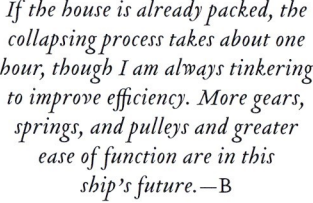

12.

11.

10.

If the house is already packed, the collapsing process takes about one hour, though I am always tinkering to improve efficiency. More gears, springs, and pulleys and greater ease of function are in this ship's future. —B

In the Wings

4.

5.

6.

The roof rests atop the house like the lid of a shoebox. Wind the wheel and the ropes pull and draw the roof upward from its pipe legs. The hinged walls, when folded for travel, are stacked with the end walls overlapping the side walls. Once the walls are up, they are bolted into place. In the wings, the floor folds down first and the roof lifts up second—caught by its hinging triangular support. Then the outer wall is slid into place, the side walls are opened on hinges, and, lastly, the seams, which meet with weather stripping, are bolted together.

7.

9.

8.

In the Wings

Living in such tight quarters means that everything needs to have a designated location. When we buy something new, we are always thinking about exactly where in the house it will live. If there isn't a spot, we make one.

For our wardrobes, I created a framework so that things could easily be added or altered. —B

Weaving the knots that will make netting inside my wardrobe's trunk. We each have two nets—one for socks and the other for underwear. —C

Using liquid gold leaf to paint details on my wardrobe drawers. —C

The two nightstands these drawers came from would have taken up twice as much space as our makeshift frame—and been twice as heavy. —B

Our original outer walls were heavy and didn't let much of a breeze pass, so we decided to design lighter ones with windows that look like French doors— we call them "windoors."

Applying the fancy wallpaper my mom thrifted for me. —C

Pre-fitting the new outer wing wall. —B

Adding cedar left over from a previous job into our cedar trunks to make shelves. FYI: Cedar repels moths and smells great! —B

Marking measurements for foam insulation with my resting grimace face. —B

When I was a kid, I loved to tinker while watching cartoons. I didn't have Legos; I had Construx, which work similarly, but create more of a framework with longer pieces (rather than the brick-like stacking pieces of Legos). There was something so relaxing about things that could be broken down and reassembled if a mistake was made.

This concept inspired our wardrobe framework. Rather than tax my mind thinking of a perfect and permanent design, I decided it'd be more fun to create a frame where things could more easily be added and altered. I used a combination of threaded black iron pipe, electrical conduit, salvaged angle iron, and wood. I love how easy it is to attach new things. —B

Our new Gnome stove from Thelin, waiting to be installed. It will be attached to a mosaic base on wheels, of course, that can move with the opening and closing of Brandon's wardrobe wall. The chimney will be piped through the upper roof and will have to be dismantled for travel.

ABOVE: *We chose a propane model instead of a woodstove because it requires less clearance, and eliminates the need to tend a fire. We can leave home and know the house is warm. It also works in a power outage. What's key is that the chimney is double walled. It draws in air through one layer to feed the flame and expels exhaust out the other, leaving the air quality inside the house unaffected. When it is lit, a warm fireplace flame is visible through the door.* OPPOSITE: *Our dream is to build respective patios off our windoors, extending our living space into nature. We picture places for friends to gather seated on vintage wicker—we've been thrifting—surrounded by potted plants, a wooden sauna, an outdoor shower, and, of course, a fire pit.* —C

There have been so many influences that have inspired my design, but two moments in film stand out.

First, in *Toy Story 2*, an old man arrives with an unfolding, contraption-rich toolbox and patiently—therapeutically—restores Woody. I wanted my workspace to evoke that vibe.

Second, the Tom Hanks character in *Joe Versus the Volcano* has the greatest steamer trunks of all time. Upright, leather, and tight as a drum, they are troves of nuanced storage, and when his ship sinks, they float him and Meg Ryan to safety. I have wanted trunk storage ever since I first saw the film.

If you look carefully left and right, you can spot the hinges for my desk and wardrobe walls. These walls are folded in first when moving. The countertop folds toward the kitchen to make way. —B

People often ask us what our style is called or how we define it. The answer is, we just buy what we like, and put it where we think it looks good. My advice when trying to develop your own style is to follow your intuition and buy what speaks to you. What does Marie Kondo say, buy what sparks joy? I may have added the buy part. —C

RIGHT: *Left of the shoe rack, you can spot the hinges for my wardrobe wall. The hinges for my desk wall are behind the pot rack. The rack, which is on wheels, must be moved before I can fold in my desk wall.* —C

A lot of people assume that Brandon and I fall into traditional gender roles—that I design everything, and Brandon builds it. On the contrary, Brandon designed a lot of what you see on these pages, and I helped build a fair amount of it. After ten years of living in this tiny home, it sometimes feels like we share one big brain, for better or for worse, and we seem to exchange ideas without communicating. I like to think Brandon and I are expanding each other's repertoires of skills, each bringing to the table what the other lacks, and learning from each other along the way. —C

A rewarding view of the wilderness near our tiny home from New Hampshire's Cardigan Mountain.

IV
BEFITTING *a* PRINCESS

Ah, the princess. No archetype is more prominent in the collective imagination of storytellers. But fancily and well-financed as these happy-ever-after creatures seem to live, surely there must be more to their appeal than their enviable stations and incredible wardrobes.

I discovered my answer in a bit of modern magic—an audiobook—I enjoyed while toiling on improvements to the chariot palace of my own princess. While listening, I found myself bending a knee of respect to the noble work of Frances Hodgson Burnett. Her masterpiece *A Little Princess* was so engaging that it grew difficult for me to pay proper attention to my tools at hand.

Unlike the typical royal tale, *A Little Princess* is the story of a princess in deed, not title. This princess espouses the virtues most befitting of a princess. More than wealth, what she possesses is unshakable dignity and grace, regardless of her situation (though she does have a fabulous wardrobe). As I listened to this story, neglectfully measuring and cutting wood and my own hands, I realized what a powerful message it conveyed. So often in life, if we aren't mindful we end up curbing our assertiveness and our personal styles for the sake of fitting undisturbedly into the low positions where others believe we belong. Our true princess, if we know how to look at her, is not simply a pretty person of privilege; she is an indomitable spirit.

I cannot think of a better way to describe the woman with whom I have shared more than fourteen years of my life. Vivacious and bold, she is and has always been an inexorable force for truth and true expression—a kaleidoscopic explosion of feminine creativity and spirit.

That got me thinking: We've been through a lot over the years, this lady and I. She has graciously endured more discomfort than any fancy woman should be asked to bear. Too long have we waded through the wilderness of unfinished furnishings and limited décor. It was time to make what wishes I could come true for her. Not all women may relate to a princess archetype, but over the years I've learned that if you are fortunate to be loved by one who does, you'd damn well better treat her like one.

OPPOSITE: *The metal flower chandelier in my office was found at the junkyard. Yeah, you heard that right—someone threw this chandelier away! Luckily, I was there to rescue it, and for only five dollars. We added white Christmas lights to it, and I couldn't be happier with my score.* —C

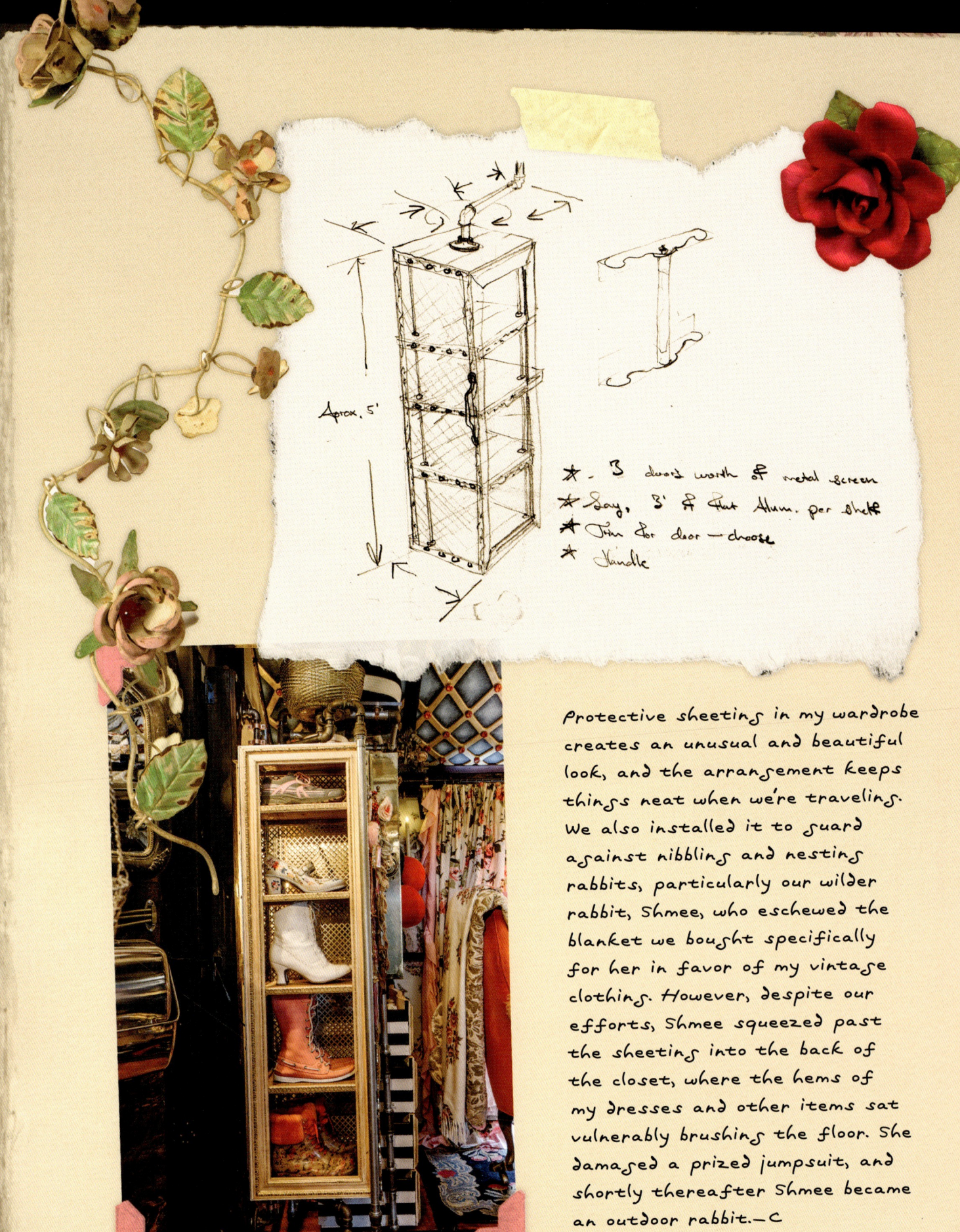

*- 3 doors worth of metal screen
* Say, 3' of flat Alum. per shelf
* Trim for door — choose
* Handle

Protective sheeting in my wardrobe creates an unusual and beautiful look, and the arrangement keeps things neat when we're traveling. We also installed it to guard against nibbling and nesting rabbits, particularly our wilder rabbit, Shmee, who eschewed the blanket we bought specifically for her in favor of my vintage clothing. However, despite our efforts, Shmee squeezed past the sheeting into the back of the closet, where the hems of my dresses and other items sat vulnerably brushing the floor. She damaged a prized jumpsuit, and shortly thereafter Shmee became an outdoor rabbit. —C

This rack rotates 360 degrees on black pipe fittings. Mounted on threaded rod, the shelves can be adjusted for different shoe heights.

I found my vanity chair for forty dollars at a flea market. It was already falling apart, and I continued to use it to death, anticipating its future makeover. When I finally got around to reupholstering it, I used the same Barbie-pink velvet I had used for my larger chair. After dismantling it, I refreshed its parts with paint and fabric, then got to work gluing, sewing, and stapling the chair back together. —C

Almost all of the fabric used on our various projects throughout the house comes from recycled or deadstock liquidators. —C

(Unnecessarily) spray-painting the base of my vintage vanity chair. —C

Cutting out a new seat base to replace the damaged one. —C

Attaching fringe trim with decorative brass nails. —C

My vanity area is filled with vintage containers, vessels, and jars. I hunt for these treasures at thrift stores and transfer my cosmetics into them. It's a meditative practice, and I enjoy the luxury of applying my serums out of these magical vessels. —C

OPPOSITE: *My wardrobe area is a mix of custom-built and found items. The pipe framework lends adaptability, while Lucite shelves add storage without making the space feel cramped. The drawers were salvaged from a set of nightstands.* ABOVE: *It was important to me to have a functional vanity area where I could apply my makeup and do my hair. We made this possible with a hodgepodge of items, including a salvaged mirror that Brandon turned into a cabinet. The pink metal cabinet above the mirror was thrifted for two dollars and reminds me of stowage in a train car. The magnetized round mirror, also thrifted, was a fun addition that cost a whopping ten dollars, and Brandon made the bookshelf from scratch.* —C

Befitting a Princess

Growing up, one of my favorite things to do was to visit yard sales and thrift shops with my mom. She would try to sneak out at five A.M., assuming nobody else in the house was awake, but she would always find me waiting by the door, ready to go. —C

We spotted this lovely chair at a thrift store for seventy-five dollars. I knew right away its flowery shape would be adorable in my office. Being novice upholsterers, we decided to leave the job to a true professional, which ended up costing us a pretty penny. We sometimes joke, why buy a new chair when you can redo a used one for the same price? —C

OPPOSITE: Although thrifted at different times and in different places, the curtains and the wallpaper appear made for each other. The wallpaper is printed with paint! RIGHT: Cherry throw pillows are the perfect accent. BOTTOM RIGHT: Braided gold trim hangs from my vanity chair, which I recovered with velvet to match the larger chair. BELOW LEFT: My floral needlework rug and footstool. I asked Brandon to add whimsical brass footed wheels to my chair. All thrifted, of course. —C

My favorite color is pink! Can you tell? It wasn't my intention for my office space to become so pink. It happened naturally. —C

OPPOSITE: Natural light filters through French doors to flood my office. In the afternoon I love to read in my chair, cozied up with thrifted throw pillows.
RIGHT: The vintage tulle ballet dress (a five-dollar find) in the window of my office tinges the light pink. The scene reminds me of the vignettes I used to linger over in the pages of Rachel Ashwell's book Shabby Chic. —C

CLOCKWISE FROM TOP LEFT: Enjoying bedtime chamomile tea. I'm lucky my wing expands to accommodate my clothing collection. Makeup lights are essential. A simple way to elevate your closet is to use matching hangers—mine are pink, of course. Whether or not drawers are exposed, painting their sides adds a lovely detail. I bought the brass Dresher trunk that is my wardrobe for twenty-five dollars at the flea market; online, it was seven hundred! Sampling my tiny perfume collection. OPPOSITE: A decorative pillow by Tamar Mogendorff that I lusted over for many months before splurging. —C

CLOCKWISE FROM TOP LEFT: Roses picked from Mom's garden. A metal rose vine winds its way through the mirror above my vanity table. Hand-painted rose details on my makeup drawer. A ceramic rose knob on my closet door. OPPOSITE, CLOCKWISE FROM TOP LEFT: An emotional support teddy bear I thrifted for five dollars and named Pearl. Thrifted plaster filigrees—I knew immediately I wanted them for the ceiling of my office. I adore tiny, collectible figurines. I store jewelry in a thrifted porcelain cameo box. —C

If it's in the tiny home or on our bodies, it's safe to assume that we sourced it secondhand or found it for free on the side of the road. We almost never (need to) buy retail.

OPPOSITE AND RIGHT: *I bought this vase at New Hampshire's Brimfield market. I couldn't leave her behind! The flowers, picked from my own backyard, resemble an idea exploding from the crown of her head. The thrifted Dale Tiffany lamp—a splurge at $75—looks straight out of the* Flower Fairies *books of my childhood.*

Of all Flowers, methinks a Rose is best.
— THE TWO NOBLE KINSMEN BY WILLIAM SHAKESPEARE AND JOHN FLETCHER

A business deal had just fallen apart. On a ride into town to run some errands, while stopped at a red light, and through my tears of mourning, I saw it. Between sobs, I said to Brandon, "There's a free desk. We should get it."

My heart is like a singing bird.
— CHRISTINA ROSSETTI

We reconstructed the desk's rectangular top in an *L*-shape to fit in the corner, added more drawers and some shelves, and painted it.

Not even a broken dream hinders my ability to spot a great roadside find.

BECOMING a MAN

Someday, if I am fortunate enough to grow very old, I will most assuredly have forgotten a great many things. I have been struggling to remember important information my entire life. This is why it is all the more peculiar for me to suggest, and I do so with a great deal of confidence, that if it ever comes to pass that all I can remember of my own story is the fairy companion by my side, I will likely still go about parroting things to her like, "I've just had an apostrophe." This line from *Hook*—wherein Robin Williams plays a grown-up Peter Pan—and indeed the film's entire script, is one of many I can recall almost photographically, unlike so many other details requisite to adulting. As I go about my day, everything I see and hear reminds me of one or another cinematic moment.

However, this talent does not always prove the most appreciated application of a man's memory, especially when, to the frustration of his partner, it seems to come at the expense of forgetting the details that she must, by default, be burdened to remember. Though I'm sure it is an oversimplification to suggest that one's brain can become so full of memories that the addition of one more can push another out, I have learned first-hand just how maddening it can be to my mate

when I don't know when the taxes are due, but I know that Bastian's mother's name in *The NeverEnding Story* is Moonchild. Or I don't know when the Zoom call is, but I have taken the time to learn the backstory behind Domingo Montoya—Inigo's father in *The Princess Bride*—who could have been a rich and famous blacksmith, by the way, but would rather have been poor and unknown than forced to make weapons for "any fool who happens along."

These aren't, of course, useless memories for a man to keep well-tended in the garden of his mind. I love these stories. The truth is that I have a tendency to recall the things that have reached my heart more easily than those that have reached my mind. But there is more to gardening than planting seeds that easily grow, and if I have learned anything from the fine films I have seen over the years, it is that it does not become a man to do only what is easy.

This was the thought that was as clearly illuminated as the silver screen in my mind one day. After I paused to consider it, and my manly duty, I decided right then and there that if trying harder to remember the unexciting information of life would lighten the wings of my partner and keep her fluttering by my side, I would dare do all I could, and more.

Fortunately, we men have more than effort at our disposal to stave off the unendurable ick of our companions; we can take the time to write things down. Organization, it seems, is the key to our salvation. What better way for a man to get started glowing-up than to commence making over his office, tidying his wardrobe, and building a finer chair from which he may more carefully ponder all the things he would be remiss to take for granted?

OPPOSITE: *I added the ring to the drafting chair I bought at a flea market—it still needs wheels. The wingback was a tattered old thing. I added ten-dollar claw feet from an estate sale. The brass wheels I thrifted for five dollars.* —B

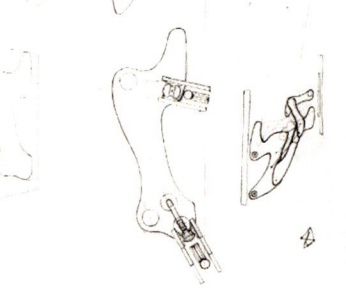
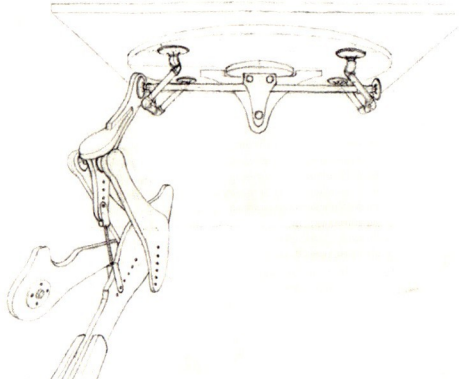
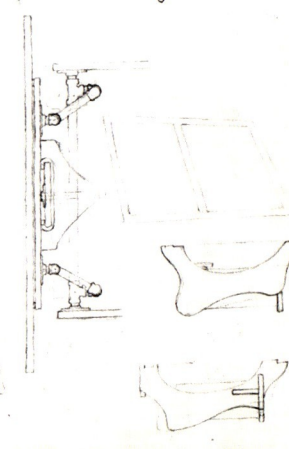

The base would slide left to right on rails.

Its tension would be adjustable.

The top would shift and pitch on black pipe.

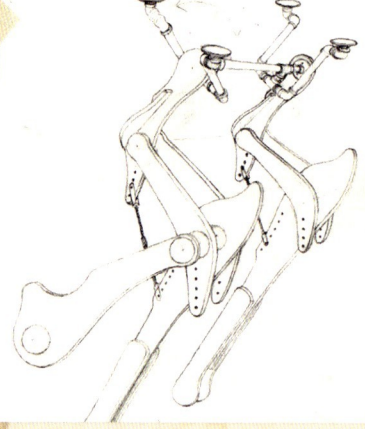
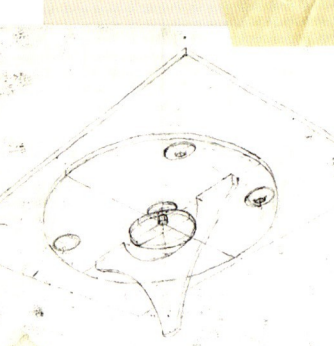
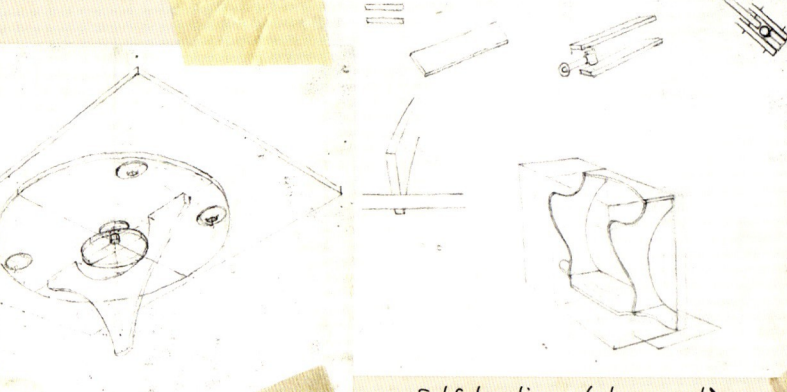

It would be counter-balanced to float on springs.

The top would swivel from portrait to landscape.

Self-leveling shelves would be mounted in the spaces all throughout the framing.

For years, I daydreamed about a desk to end all desks: Megadesk. It would move in every direction—a writing-painting-drawing-workbench all built into one alien-like contraption of wood, metal bandings, nuts and bolts, and pipe. —B

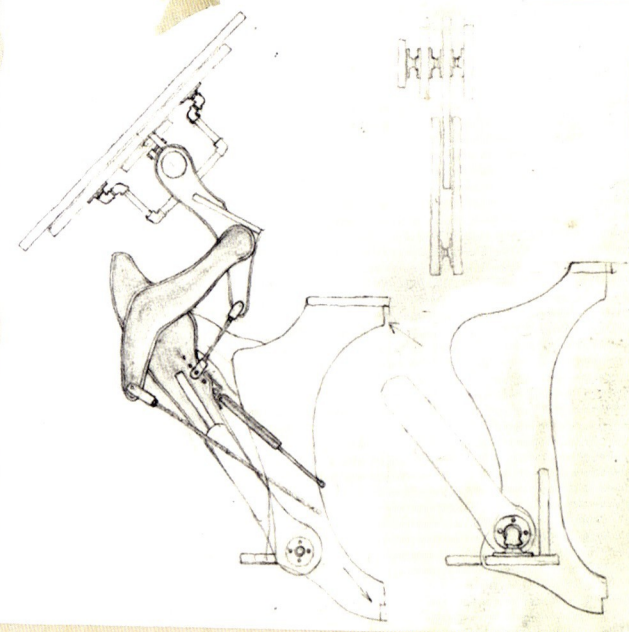

It would take up a lot of space.

One winter, when the time finally came to manifest this marvel I had thought about for so long, I prepared to set to work making my dream a reality, only to realize that somewhere along the course of my years of pining I had completely lost interest. —B

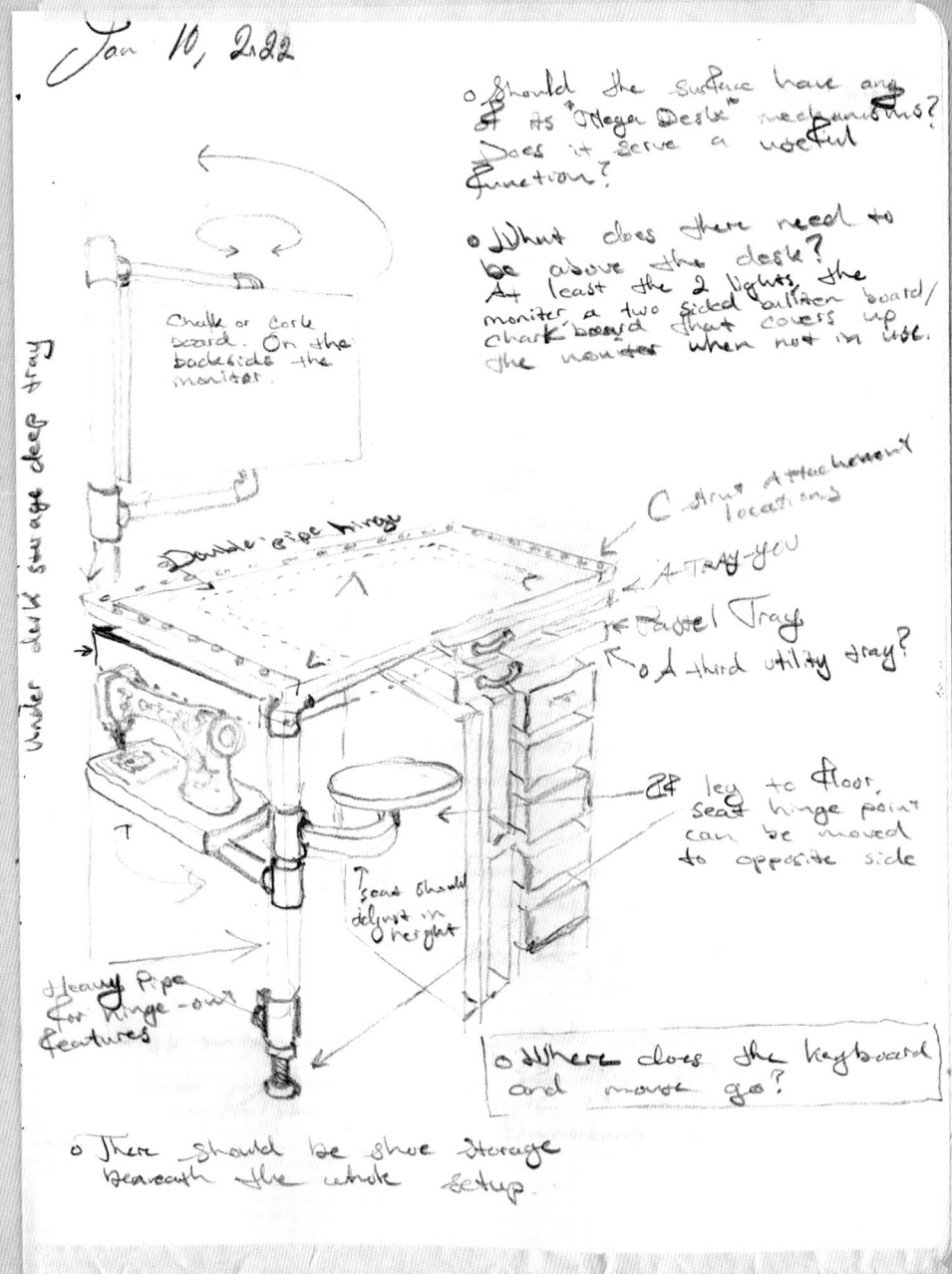

A sketch of how I imagined my simpler desk.

At first, I chastised myself for not following through. But the more I thought about it, the more I realized Megadesk didn't fit the feel of our house (or fit into our house, period). I love the idea of making things from scratch, but the tiny house had always been about fun and fast upcycle projects. We'd find something interesting that could be quickly transformed into something useful, install it, love it, and then we'd move on. Lately, the projects had been growing more time-consuming, and there didn't seem to be enough room just to enjoy living. A soothing image of something simpler crept into my mind: an old-fashioned desk, the kind where an elderly watchmaker might sit. I began quietly to hope that such a thing might cross my path. —B

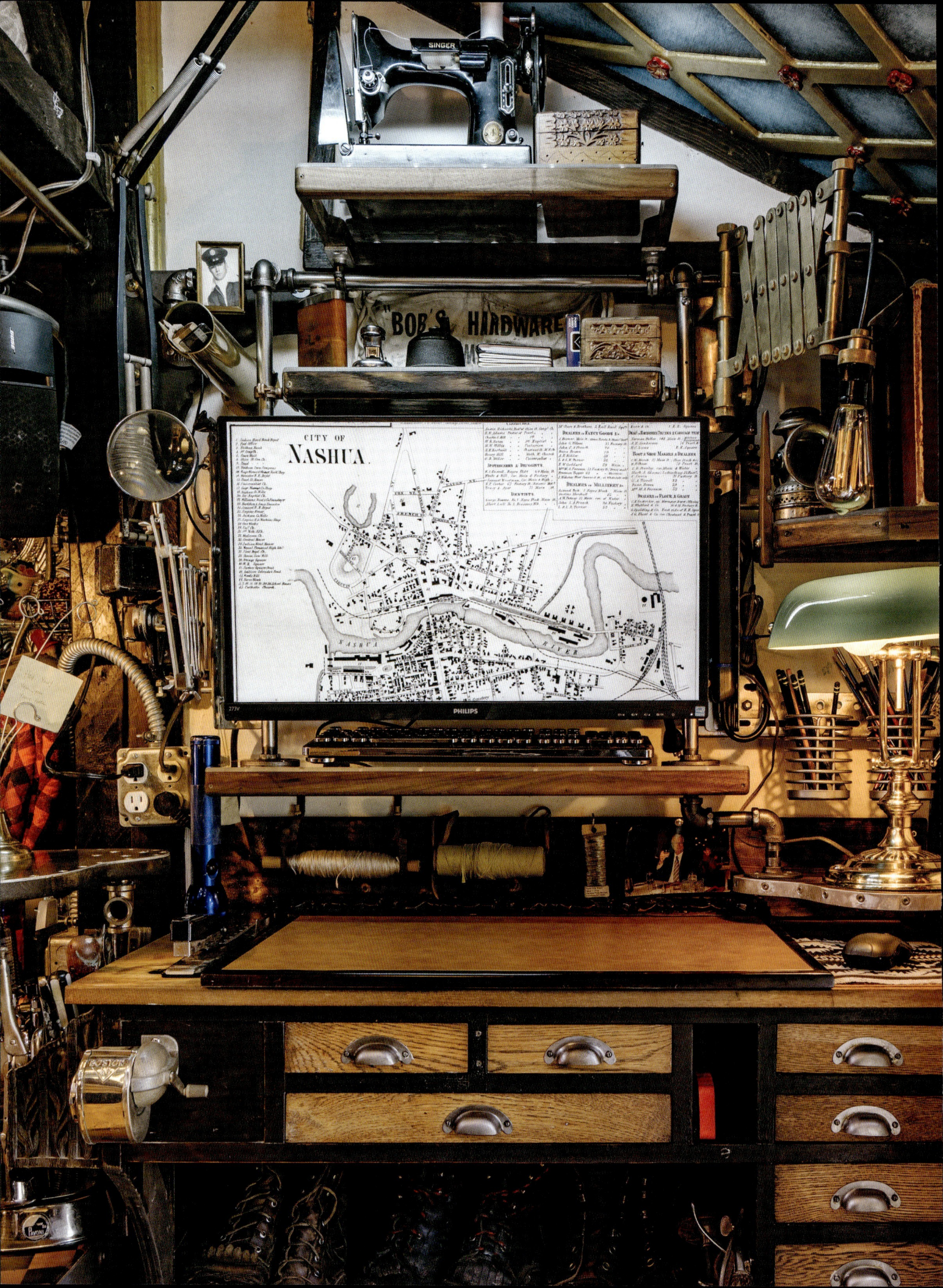

Furniture should invite you. If you aren't using it, there's a strong chance that something about it is awkward. My new desk is a sanctuary. I have to pull myself away from it.

OPPOSITE: *The great thing about having a clear vision of something is that it will stand out to you when you happen upon it. I happened upon this desk while shopping for an interior design job. I trimmed its lower left side into a curve, Chloe stained it light and dark, I affixed it to my hinging wall, and then I added every contraption I could imagine. I add more every chance I get. Polished black pipe serves as the framework for shelves I made of acrylic glass and wood. I made the library lamp (right) and the aluminum food tray (left) to swivel on black pipe flanges. I use maps of my old stomping grounds as ambient screensavers.* —B

We've found that the more details that accumulate, the more the eye has to process. The effect is a sense of the space being larger. Our house never looked smaller than when it was completely empty. —B

LEFT AND OPPOSITE: I combined a desk magnifying lens with the retractable arm of a broken lamp. BELOW LEFT: I thrifted these cups for seventy-five cents each. BELOW RIGHT: This envelope-organizer-turned-tool-caddy is actually plastic. —B

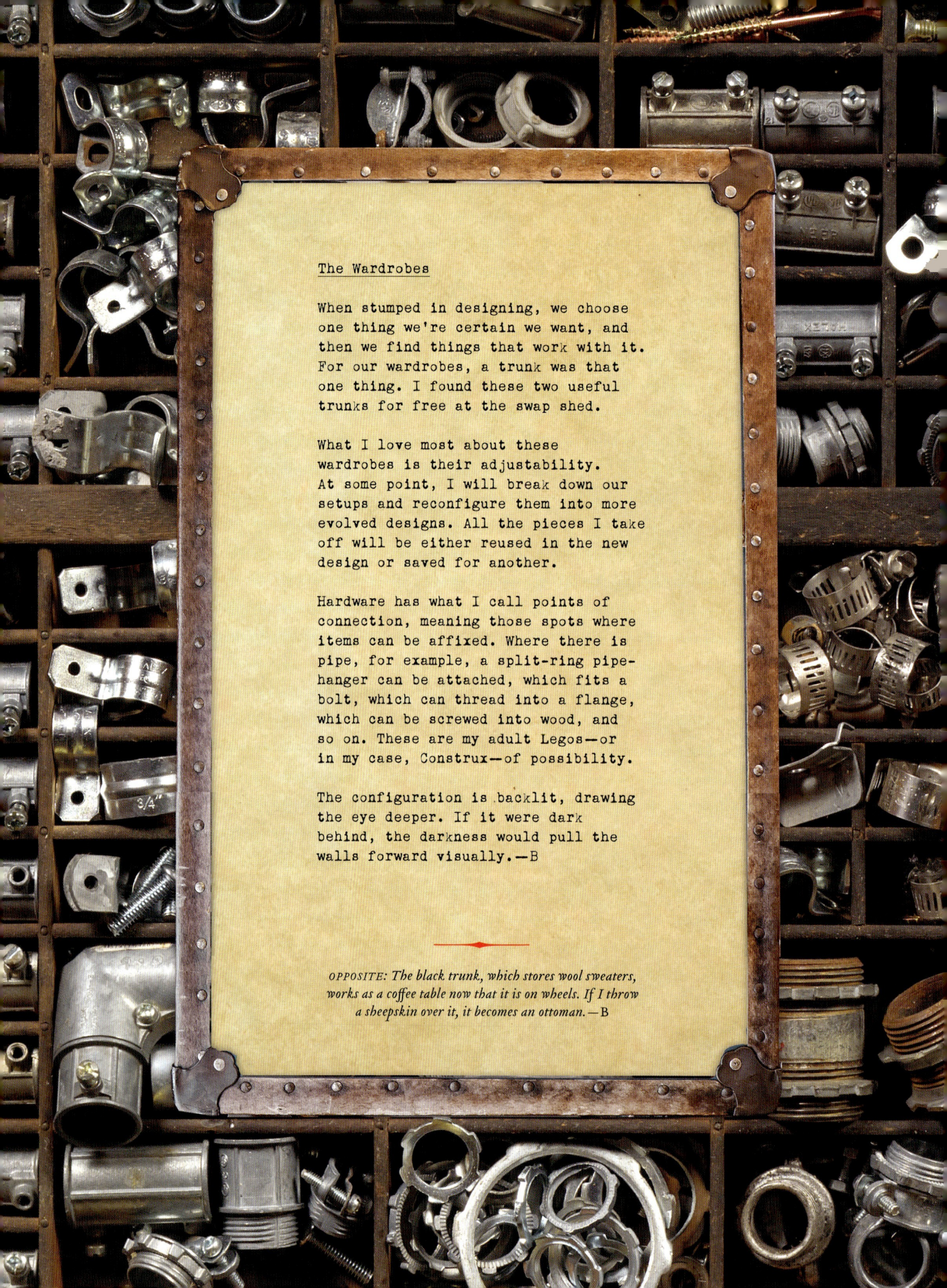

The Wardrobes

When stumped in designing, we choose one thing we're certain we want, and then we find things that work with it. For our wardrobes, a trunk was that one thing. I found these two useful trunks for free at the swap shed.

What I love most about these wardrobes is their adjustability. At some point, I will break down our setups and reconfigure them into more evolved designs. All the pieces I take off will be either reused in the new design or saved for another.

Hardware has what I call points of connection, meaning those spots where items can be affixed. Where there is pipe, for example, a split-ring pipe-hanger can be attached, which fits a bolt, which can thread into a flange, which can be screwed into wood, and so on. These are my adult Legos—or in my case, Construx—of possibility.

The configuration is backlit, drawing the eye deeper. If it were dark behind, the darkness would pull the walls forward visually. —B

OPPOSITE: The black trunk, which stores wool sweaters, works as a coffee table now that it is on wheels. If I throw a sheepskin over it, it becomes an ottoman. —B

In such a small space, it's essential for everything to have its own place. When something doesn't have a home, it meanders around like the odd man out in a game of musical chairs and gets in the way. —B

OPPOSITE: *I added these cedar shelves to my trunk, which was already cedar lined. With individual shirt slots, I'm living the dream.* ABOVE: *I added the boot and moccasin shelves beneath my desktop. Stray shoes used to loiter everywhere.* —B

Becoming a Man

Upholstering

I've long had an interest in upholstering. When I was twenty, I had an idea of making couches that come apart for moving, but naively I went to Building #19 to see what people were paying for couches, saw they were selling for four hundred dollars each, and deduced in my blue-collar innocence that I couldn't compete. I would later learn that Building #19 was essentially a thrift store, and that there are actually people out there with disposable income who will pay for handmade quality.

Fabric faux leather—a product made from recycled leather scraps bonded to fabric—salvaged military buttons, decorative brass nails, and Chesterfield-style tufting testify to the fact that I was watching a lot of Sherlock Holmes (the 1980s series starring Jeremy Brett) when I set out to reupholster a dusty old chair that Chloe bought for twenty-five dollars. I am thoroughly thankful for the learning experience, and I feel quite capable of doing the job better when next I try my hand, but I'm afraid my chance is coming sooner rather than later, as the recycled leather I used began tearing and falling apart within a month of my applying it. The product is a noble idea, but having learned my lesson, I would look into any material thoroughly before using it. —B

A good way to get started learning to upholster is to take a piece apart and see how it's constructed. It's a patient person's game, but I found it to be a peaceful experience. —B

I attached table legs to my makeshift base. —B

There are upholstering tools that can save time and your hands. A stitch in time... —B

I used a burlap coffee sack on the seat back to save money. —B

Christine McConnell has a very helpful episode regarding tufting on her show From the Mind of Christine McConnell. —B

One of the things I wish I had learned before trying tufting—making diamond-shaped folds in the leather—is that the diamond pattern in the leather must be a little larger than the one in the foam or the tufts don't fluff up in the middle. You can see in the image opposite that mine are drawn quite tight. —B

Adding the decorative nails was my favorite part—watching an amorphous item transform more into furniture with each nail. —B

My thrifted color scheme seems to have sorted me into the house of Gryffindor, which isn't far off, as our illusion of space is a magic trick we're always trying to perfect. —B

CLOCKWISE FROM TOP LEFT: I named my rotating shelf A-Tray-You after the main character in The NeverEnding Story. It uses a black pipe flange as a hinge. A twelve-dollar thrifted light. All of the curtain elements were separately thrifted, down to the rings, so it was a pleasure to see them come together. OPPOSITE: The chair needed to be on wheels so that it can be moved easily when it's time to access the wardrobe. —B

There isn't much I find more rejuvenating than a well-supplied camping experience, away from my phone. —B

Checklist for a Happier Camper

What could be more relaxing than camping properly? Some of you are laughing, but if you don't like camping I'd bet there's a traumatic experience sullying your impression. Hard ground? A wet tent? Freezing cold? All of the above? Oh, dear.

If you're interested in giving camping another shot, here are some suggestions to turn a merely tolerable camping experience into an enjoyable one. It's not comprehensive; it's a list of luxuries to add to your essentials.

Color Palette: Earth tones give a site an elevated, old-fashioned feel that harmonizes with the environment. The mood we try to set is one inspired by old campaign furniture. Pops of color can be fun, but keep 'em on a leash. Blue tarps are great for being seen by search planes, but not so great for setting the mood.

Awning: An awning guarantees you a dry place to work, and play, even in the rain. Ours is a 16-by-20-foot waxed canvas tarp; I built poles for it out of two-by-fours.

Lighting: Safely position tiki torches, and your site will glow pleasantly and be easier to navigate at night. Bug repelling torch oil does wonders. LED tea lights are also a pretty way to further illuminate walking paths. Hang simple, reliable, quiet oil lamps in choice places outside. Battery lamps are great inside the tent. You could also try battery powered fairy lights, inside or out. Headlamps are great for reading (try spooky books) and are an all-around useful camp tool.

Big Tent: Having a little more room goes a long way. Waterproofing spray or detergent will upkeep a new tent, or make an old one functional again.

Get Off the Ground: The ground is not only uncomfortable, but it conducts the heat out of your body. Air mattresses are at risk of popping—use discretion. Consider cots and pads together.

Extra Blankets: Great for sleeping, and cozying up by the fire.

Pillows: A rolled-up jacket may work for backpacking, but this is camping. Pillows for bed, pillows for chairs.

Artisanal Marshmallows: There are mom-and-pop companies that make wonderful small-batch marshmallows with incredible flavor for truly delicious s'mores.

Propane Stove: Be sure to bring a big pot to heat water on the stove.

Washing Up: For washing dishes, in addition to that hot water, make things easier by bringing two big tubs—one for washing dishes, the other for rinsing—plus some biodegradable soap and a drying rack.

Chairs, Side Tables, and Footrests: For less than one hundred dollars, we've thrifted eight chairs and a handful of side tables and footrests, all wooden. Throw a sheepskin and blanket on for the royal treatment.

Music: Bring a battery powered speaker that you can plug into your phone. We're always adding to the multiple camping playlists we curate. If you use two speakers, you can put them on opposite sides of the site, which allows you to hear better and keep the volume lower. As an added bonus, your neighbors may appreciate the quiet.

Tip: Think outside the box. The things you collect don't need to be made for camping to be great for camping.

VI

the KITCHEN of TOMORROW

When I was a child, and streaming was called television, there was a hilariously inappropriate cartoon that would occasionally interrupt my morning dose of *Tom & Jerry* called *The House of Tomorrow*. This bit of satire from 1949 poked fun at the live action promotional films of the day, taking every new futuristic home design that manufacturers had been touting—you know the type: "even junior here will love doing his dishes in this dishwasher of the future!"—and putting an absurd spin on it, like an automatic sandwich-maker that shuffles meat and bread and deals out sandwiches like playing cards. Some of these inventions came in versions for each of the household's stereotypes: one for the man, one for the wife, one for the child, and, lastly, one for the dreaded mother-in-law, which was always a sinister device.

I share this story for two reasons. The first is that long before we ever dreamed of a bold renovation of our entire kitchen (the details of which comprise this chapter), back in the early days when we undertook putting it together piecemeal from this or that, we had no idea that our kitchen would end up looking so retro-futuristic. Second, somewhere during the process of transforming this kitchen from a simple collection of roadside finds to the functional sphere of cooking convenience it is today, I found myself, for a moment, just a moment, thinking of the cartoon when my mother-in-law walked through our door one day with some casual words of advice.

Allow me to explain.

When I began designing our house, I had the lofty aspiration of directing rainwater from our roof to our gutters into two elevated barrels, and then allowing gravity to feed the water into the plumbing lines. In theory, that would allow us to live anywhere that it rains. The main trouble with my plan, aside from some of its more obvious shortcomings, like winter's freezing temperatures, was that the natural pressure the water exerted grew weaker the farther the water traveled. The solution? Keep all plumbing close to the barrels. This meant that the kitchen sink, the shower, and—brace yourself—even the bathroom, would all reside in the kitchen. To make room, we awkwardly placed our refrigerator on the other side of the house.

"This sounds absurd!" I can hear some of you say. "Get a water pump!" And I'm inclined to agree with you . . . now. But the me of then had only a few junk finds and fifty dollars to make the kitchen. So, we made the kitchen, and we framed the bathroom in its corner. Chloe took pains to stencil its walls beautifully, and I built a composting toilet and installed a bathroom sink. We salvaged an oversized shutter and fitted it like a saloon door, cut up and painted a metal case to use as our medicine cabinet, and then, after some time passed, got a water pump. I tiled the bathroom floor, which was a lot of work, and the reason we put the bathroom in the kitchen in the first place had blissfully faded from our memories—until—my mother-in-law came to visit one day and said, "It looks nice, but I would have put the refrigerator where the bathroom is and the bathroom where the refrigerator is."

OPPOSITE: *Raising the main floor for our unfolding wings resulted in a step down into the kitchen, which distinguishes it nicely from the main area without separating it. This makes cooking interactive and more fun. An adjustable arm allows Brandon's monitor to face the kitchen so we can watch a show while we cook.*

After using the kitchen for a few years, we understood what we truly wanted from the space. We needed more counter area, a dishrack conducive to washing dishes, room for our appliances, lots of food storage, and maybe even a little decor. —C

Using wood filler in the tiny gaps of the checkered butcher block countertop Brandon made from a mixture of black walnut and maple.

This black pipe framework, spraypainted chrome color, holds the under-cabinet dish storage.

Our old kitchen, for reference. The bathroom was behind the shutter-made door to the left. —C

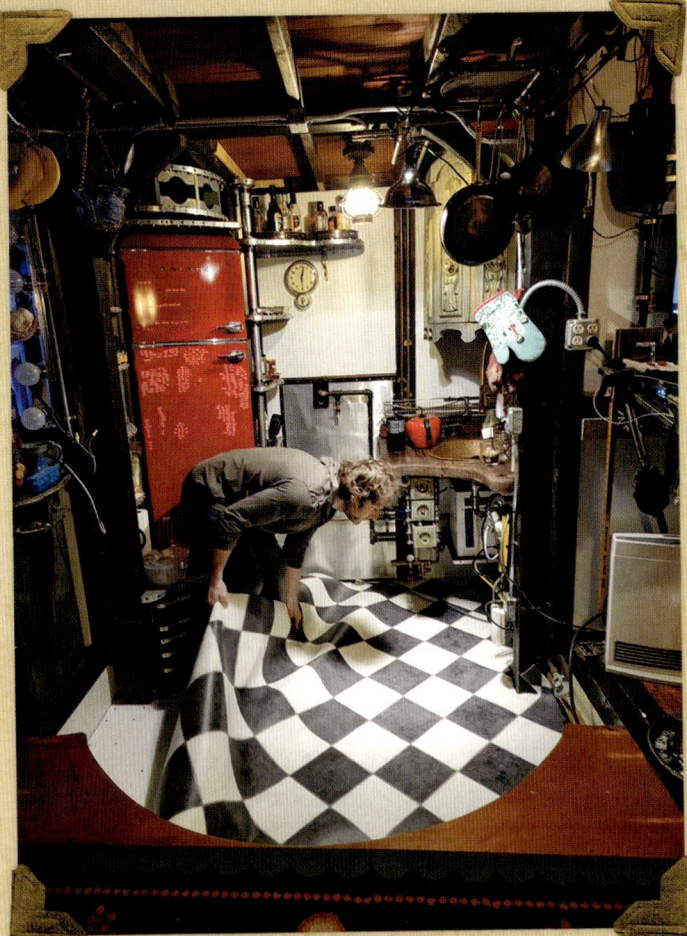

We used this fun black-and-white vinyl sheet for the kitchen floor. It took months to install, but not because it was difficult. No, the actual installation was simple enough. The difficulty arose because in a state of over-worked delirium, we accidentally cut the shape upside down, and we had to scrap it. After a long nap, we reordered the same flooring for take two. We used the scrap for our bathroom. The rest we'll use somewhere, someday.

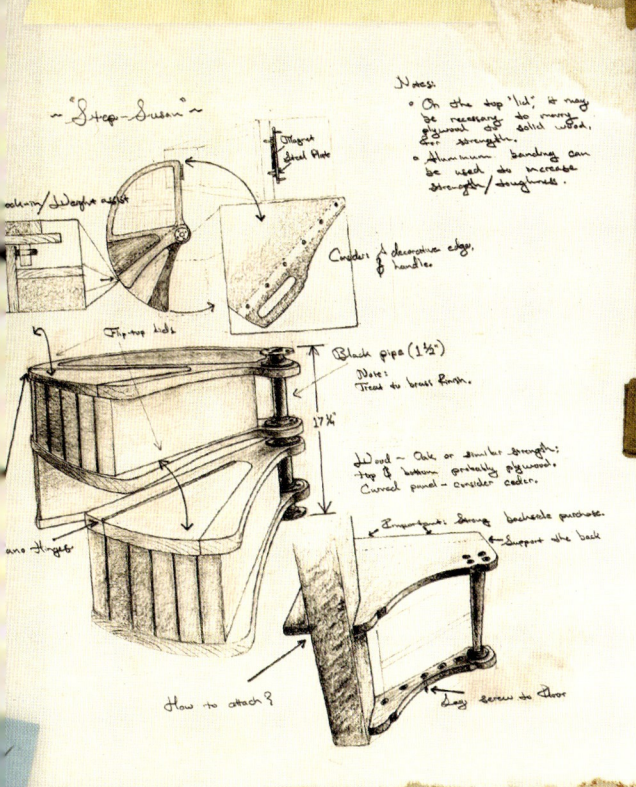

The aluminum is mostly bendable by hand, and a hammer and torch help in tricky spots.

This rotating wine rack has mostly turned into a sparkling water rack.

I added aluminum banding to the organic, flowing edges of the wood. It creates a kind of futuristic medieval look, and it makes the wood edges much more durable. —B

We wanted the fridge off the ground for easier use, which created a natural space for a lazy Susan, but we also needed a step. Enter not-so-lazy Susan. She serves as both.

I used black pipe—which I brass plated—as the hinge for the not-so-lazy Susan. —B

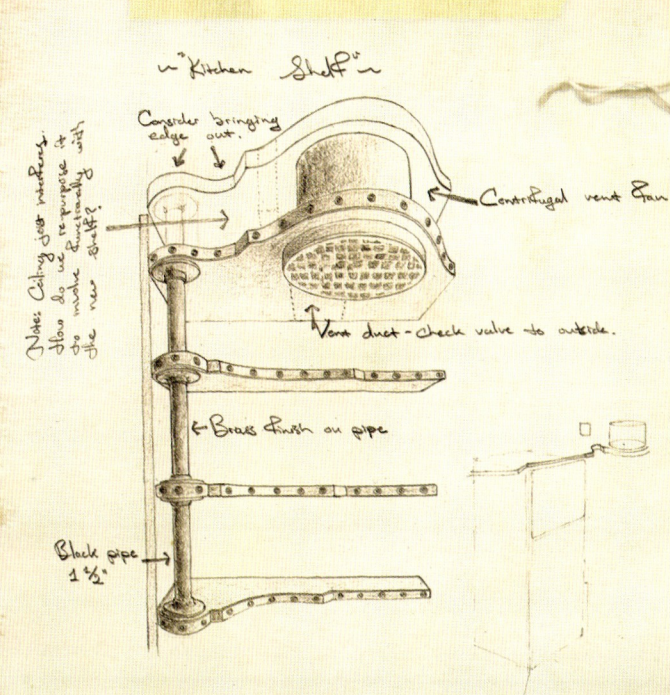

We shop locally at farmstands and co-ops as much as we can. We aspire to have a property where we can grow our own food and flowers and even raise our own chickens for eggs.

OPPOSITE: *The kitchen is the heart of our tiny house.* ABOVE: *We originally titled this chapter "Make Way for the Sous Chef," because the renovation, particularly this countertop, would make room for an assistant chef in the kitchen. The reality, however, is that the second person is always a little underfoot. We take turns.*

The Kitchen of Tomorrow

Our design philosophy is to work from big to small and knowns to unknowns. The big piece we started with in our kitchen was our white vintage Magic Chef oven. It's the anchor that inspired every additional piece of decor. Sometimes, the anchor isn't big; it's just the only thing you're certain you like. It's the known.

OPPOSITE: This countertop leg is a bedpost, one of a set gifted to us by our friends Lynn and Gerhard. We show as much floor as we can because it makes the space feel larger. RIGHT: The step on the not-so-lazy Susan was tricky to design, and I doubted it would work until the moment I stood on it. To my satisfaction, it is rock solid. —B

CLOCKWISE FROM TOP LEFT: Brandon and I met at Starbucks, where I worked as a barista, so making and enjoying coffee has always been a tradition of ours. Can you believe I almost didn't purchase this three-dollar strawberry-shaped teakettle at the thrift store because I wondered whether it was too childish? Preparing Cornish game hens to roast. I thrifted the perfect grease crock, on-theme with strawberries. We make most of our meals from scratch at home and split the responsibility of cooking. Homemade strawberry shortcake, yum! OPPOSITE: Whipping up some batter for mini-waffles. —C

This pantry under our kitchen step was originally a "rabbitat" for our two adopted, indoor, free-range rabbits.

In the kitchen, we wanted to create a spherical space encircled by a curving perimeter of resources. Hanging pots, glassware, and fruit baskets around the periphery helped define the area without isolating it from the rest of the house.

ABOVE: *This charming metal sconce cost ten dollars at my favorite estate sale ever: the strawberry lady sale (see page 200 for more)! We adorned our own strawberry patch by proudly mounting this light, which changes the whole mood of the kitchen when lit.* OPPOSITE: *Our vintage 1950s Magic Chef stove was a lucky find on Craigslist. We paid 150 dollars for it—a steal, as it had spent the better part of two decades unused in a basement.*

The Kitchen of Tomorrow

I have always loved the idea of combining dish drying and storage. It's a model of efficiency that makes doing dishes so much easier. For a year, I collected all manner of chrome, copper, and brass storage pieces. I then riveted leftover aluminum scraps from our roof to create a backsplash with drip pan that leads to the sink. I used black pipe that I painted chrome—though I later wised up and bought galvanized pipe—to make the framework to which all the pieces are attached. —B

LEFT: *The "CHICKEN FARMER I STILL LOVE YOU" mug, which denizens of New Hampshire might recognize, is the only piece here not thrifted. The hand-pounded sink, which our friend picked up overseas, awaited a purpose in his basement for years, until he realized we had been wishing for just such a thing.* —C

Romanticizing your life means taking ordinary moments and pulling the beauty from them. Of course, in reality this isn't always possible. However, it certainly became easier for us when we began cultivating a living space that is purposefully romantic.

LEFT: Elevating the fridge made it easier to peek into its lower shelves, and the not-so-lazy Susan's storage can be peered into from above.
OPPOSITE: *We take time to appreciate the little things.*

I have a weakness for whimsically shaped Dutch ovens and other pots. When I'm pulling a pumpkin-shaped crock out of the oven, it makes me feel like an enchanted mouse living her best life in a stump in the woods—straight out of a Beatrix Potter tale.—C

OPPOSITE AND ABOVE: *We have learned that indirect lighting—there are LED cords that run through our cabinetry—draws your eyes deeply into recesses, which gives the illusion of more space.*

The Kitchen of Tomorrow

Throughout 2020, while everyone was cleaning out their closets, Brandon and I were on a total thrifting binge—really a pillage. With thrifting and hiking our only activities, we became slightly addicted to what we lovingly named the haul high. During this time, we collected lots of dishes and accessories for our kitchen. Just because we live in a tiny home, I didn't want to sacrifice the opportunity to have a cookie jar, or a cute tea set, or a sake set! Or the ability to entertain friends or cook a Thanksgiving meal. Brandon was able to create the clever shelves next to our fridge that beautifully display our dishes and kitchenware. Although it requires a bit of work to pack all of this up when we travel, I think it's worth the trade-off. —C

Some of my favorite kitchen items: My collection of Baileys winking teacups, thrifted for a few dollars each. The clock was twenty dollars at our favorite thrift store. We didn't know we needed its timer until we started using it. The his-and-hers 1950s chalkware bluebirds to the right were thrifted for two dollars and fifty cents each! Brandon made these lazy Susans from thrifted silver trays. —C

The tiny house necessitates a more natural beauty regimen for me, and for that I am thankful. Because our graywater system demands that we use biodegradable products, I find myself in better alignment with the planet.

Before I had access to the latest Internet trends and hacks, I read the book The Natural Way to Super Beauty by Mary Ann Crenshaw. First published in 1974, this book introduced me to the concept that what we put in our bodies is as important as what we put on them. To this day, I use it as the foundational philosophy of my current practices—some concepts simply don't age.

Since then, I've learned that manuka honey makes a great antimicrobial face mask, both banana peels and potato wedges work well as a facial resurfacing toner, rosemary oil on the scalp stimulates hair growth, batana oil has a molecular structure small enough to penetrate the hair shaft for superior shine and strength, and beef tallow mixed with essential oils makes the best moisturizer. I can't wait to discover more.—C

OPPOSITE: Picking blueberries on a hillside in Vermont in a sustainably made dress by New Hampshire designer House of Marrow.

VII

the OLD CAPTAIN'S VANITY

We humans have a great gift for not thinking. That sounds like a cynical cliché, I know, but I mean it sincerely. I sometimes wonder how difficult life's greater concerns would be if we busy folk had to go about concentrating on every trifling task. Instead, we learn to do something, and, with a little practice, the skill becomes ingrained in us, automatic even. This aptitude carries on beyond walking and chewing bubble gum; we are likewise blessed with power of formed opinion. We are happy to learn a thing, like the fact that this tea I freshly poured is too hot to drink; I needn't curiously swallow it, again, to find out.

Unfortunately, there is a downside to this contemplative shortcut, and it reveals itself when one, like a sailor, sets his course on an idea and fails to adjust it when new information is made ready. We sail onward assured that our trajectory was soundly plotted, that our decision was thoughtfully made, but the course, redirected by new, unacknowledged details, especially if it be a long one, may, by the slightest error in degree, lead us somewhere unintended.

Such was the case with the old captain's vanity. It was the result of a first failed attempt to craft a simple washbasin and mirror. Chloe and I envisioned it on a day when a sprinkling of whiskers by her makeup mirror made it clear there was no proper place for me to trim the wisdom from my beard, our original bathroom being too compact and awkwardly designed to fit a suitable grooming mirror.

One of the remarkable benefits of working alongside one's spouse is that after some time ideas needn't really be shared; they kind of spring up together in the minds of both at once. This was the case with our envisioned vanity. Chloe and I both imagined the kind of old sink that in the time before plumbing might have been in the bedroom of a gentleman. Or better yet, it could be the kind of station one might find in the captain's chamber aboard a sailing ship of times passed.

It is hard to say where we went off course with our original vanity. By degrees, our interior design had been quietly evolving. We had only recently considered moving our bathroom out of the kitchen, and we hadn't yet realized that the only place our charming new parlor stove could functionally belong was beside my wardrobe. So, that's where I placed a clumsy sink against its will.

In retrospect, our relocated and better designed bathroom was the obvious location to place our frustrated old vanity, which is what we eventually did. That observation would have been a logical conclusion, and I would have reached it sooner had I stopped, looked around, and considered the course anew. But I did not. Instead, like Ahab hunting the white whale, I had long forgotten to consider whether my plan was a reasonable one. When I was finished, and the protruding, clumsy spectacle I had built was before my eyes, and the eyes of my mate, I knew that all my labor had been in vain.

OPPOSITE: I read a feng shui book a lifetime ago and retained two things. One, don't sleep with your head toward the doorway; it feels vulnerable, and you won't rest easily. And two, octagonal rooms are pleasing. When you walk through them, there's an enjoyable flow. We applied this principle by placing our bathroom wall on a diagonal angle. Our new and improved captain's vanity is right at home here.

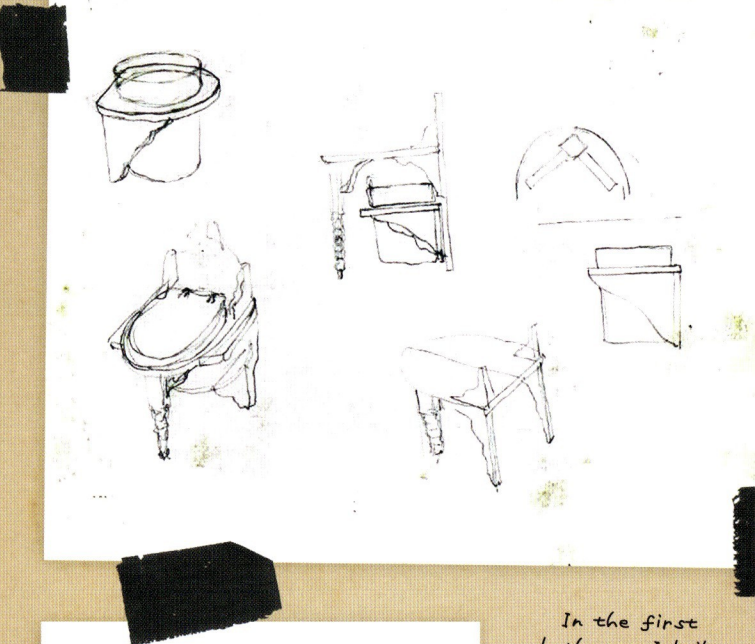

In the first bathroom, I built three iterations of a composting toilet to fit where a store-bought one wouldn't. —B

Staining and sealing the wood with polyurethane really brought out the texture of its surface. —C

I inherited my dad's hardware when he passed. I love making new things out of materials he left behind. It feels like he's still lending a hand. —B

Having gone so alien with our kitchen renovation, we thought it'd be nice to anchor our home design by bringing more of an old ship feel to our bathroom project. We had some chunky salvaged barn boards left over from a job. I ripped them into thinner boards on the table saw, shaved character into their surface with a block plane, and pieced them together with whatever hardware I could find on my shelf. —B

Jazzing up these plain modern hinges by cutting some old-fashioned curves into them.

The staining and painting jobs usually fall under my jurisdiction, a purgatory of sorts. —C

A folding wash sink. This is actually new—rare in our house.

There tends to be a post-apocalyptic romantic quality to our projects. We're always digging up forgotten old things and turning them into something new. —B

The failed old captain's vanity. I tried. —B

Turkey roaster medicine cabinet.

There are definitely some medieval vibes in this design.

I love how the light picks up the details in the wood's surface. I created these grooves with a block plane— a trick I learned from our friend Chance. Modern materials are often too perfect; I am starved for evidence of handwork in carpentry, the effect of which is illustrated here. It's an homage to simpler times. —B

OPPOSITE: *Folding wash sinks were common on old trains and ships. We hoped to find a vintage one, but they proved very expensive. This modern equivalent does the job nicely, and nods to the kitchen's retro vibe.*
RIGHT: *The brass mermaid medallion on the bathroom door came from an antique store for twenty-five dollars. We think it used to be a lid for a jewelry box.*

Little touches keep the bathroom pretty: a gilt mirror, a rose-covered box, rabbit-embroidered hand towels.

ABOVE: Bathroom meets broom closet. Rather than hide from the fact that the space is small, we decided to highlight it. OPPOSITE: The old saw is true—mirrors really do create a sense of more space. There's so much going on in the large mirror; it gives your mind a place to tarry. —B

The Old Captain's Vanity

LEFT: *We are always hunting for brass in thrift stores and scored this darling gem for five dollars.* OPPOSITE: *The skull painting comes from actor/artist Eric Lutes. We've had the pleasure of working with him on a few films, and we've also rented his paintings for set dressing. In appreciation, he gifted us this spooky piece. A brass fireplace tool hanger holds our brooms and brushes—and cost just one dollar. Chloe plans to paint the upper shelf in a folk pattern. It's on the list.*

I am always on the hunt for pretty containers. I fill them with our cleaning and bath products. —C

OPPOSITE: *Our plated brass train rack is made by Restoration Hardware. It was a thrift store score at eighteen dollars!* ABOVE: *We wanted an incinerating toilet but couldn't find one small enough to fit, so Brandon built this composting toilet (his fourth attempt). Inside, he fit a fiberglass diverter that sends liquids forward (into a storage tank) and the solid matter back. Solid matter is then buried under proper cover materials that are kept in the colonial trash can above. Odorless, it dries out quickly and turns to fertile soil once transported to a holding tank outside. Tip: The scent of urine is neutralized by a dash of vinegar.* —C

The Old Captain's Vanity

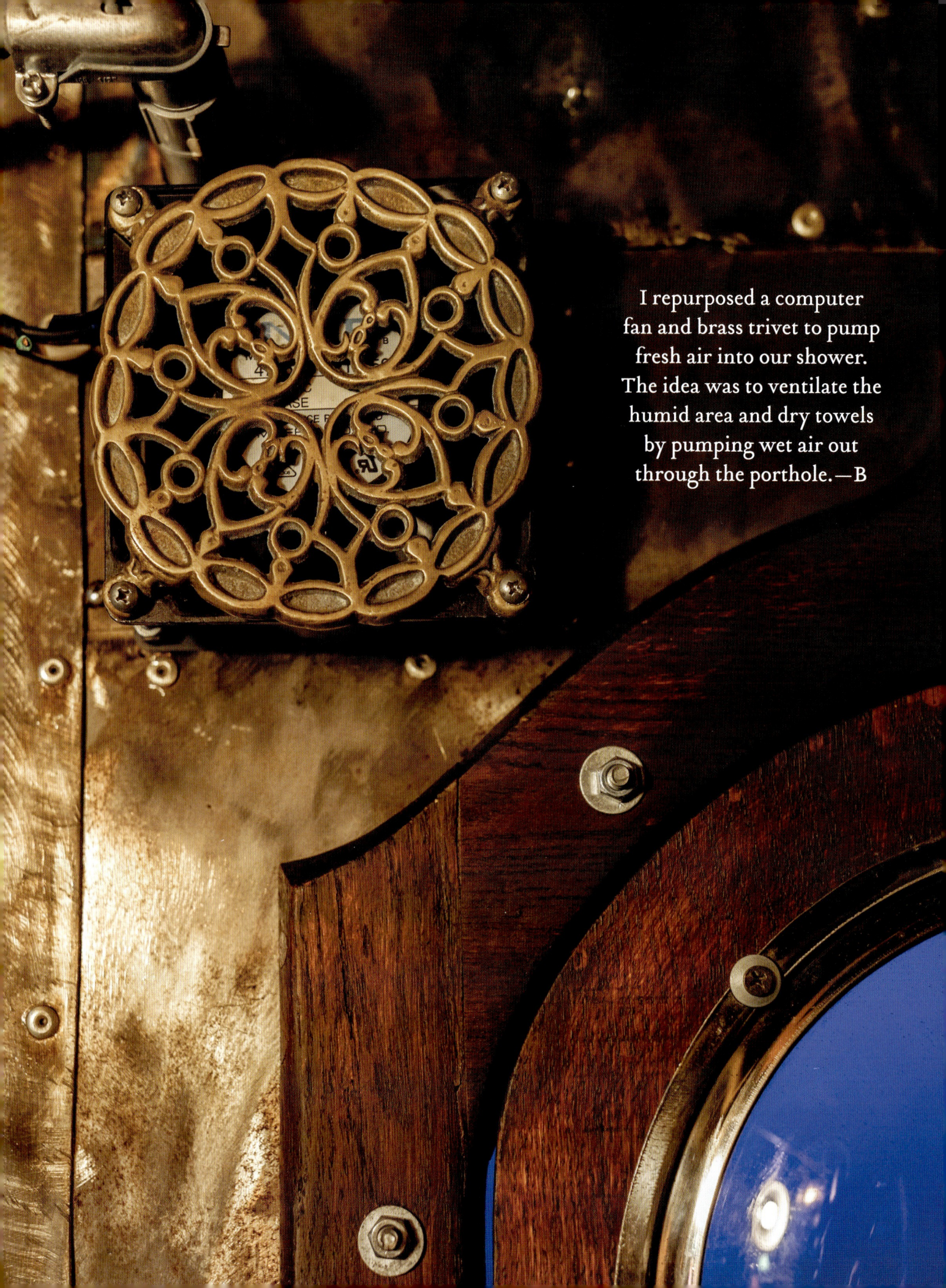

I repurposed a computer fan and brass trivet to pump fresh air into our shower. The idea was to ventilate the humid area and dry towels by pumping wet air out through the porthole. —B

On our shower door is a budget porthole window made from a crockpot lid. Brandon found the lid in a heap of unloved wreckage outside a junk shop in Maine and asked, "How much?" The shop owner replied, "One dollar!" — C

This brass porthole, whose twin is on the outside of the house, came from a junkyard in Maine. The owner wanted eighty dollars for the pair, but we didn't have the cash. Later, after replacing the leaf springs on our trailer, we took them to the junkyard. The same gentleman exclaimed, "I've been looking for a set of those! How about I trade you the porthole windows you were looking at for them?" — C

OPPOSITE: *Our medicine cabinet is made from free materials we found at the town swap shed. The mirror came first. Later, Brandon came across a turkey-roasting pan and knew he could combine the two. Resourceful!*

We built this shower out of twenty dollars in scrap metal we bought from the junkyard. Inspired by silvery riveted airplanes from the 1940s and old submarine doors, I cut the miscellaneous pieces into patchwork sizes, drilled holes, and riveted and bolted pieces together. The door you see is the second iteration. The first I made of plywood, but it didn't last. The new one is white oak and is holding up quite well. We painted the outside of the shower with a clear coat, so the metal pieces don't rust. Tip: There are tub and tile paints you can buy that are extremely tenacious, so you don't have to paint the inside of your shower a hundred times, like we did. —B

VIII
TALL TALES

Fairy tale—I wonder if there is any more commonplace idea seeded in the earliest memories of us all. Folktales first passed down by word of mouth, fairy tales have been shepherding humanity away from treacherous paths and pitfalls for ages immemorial. These ancient yarns, like song, are such an old tradition that it's hard to imagine when they may have first sprouted and taken wing from one captive listener to another, but of this we can be certain: of all the subjects these stories relate, there are none more ubiquitous nor cherished than that of true love.

But what is true love? And better yet, does it ever truly last? There are more tales of lovers coming together than we can count, but how many stories have you heard that tell of soulmates, not merely falling in love but actually living out their years in love? It seems to me that "happily ever after" is more easily described in three words than it can be in many more. Slightly off-topic for a book about a house, but I've recently found myself contemplating long, lasting love.

Perhaps that is because just as fairy tales tell a more pleasant story with each new rendition, in this book the image of our life is shown from the most pleasing view. As you can imagine, this is generally to our liking, but it's a sunny presentation that, alone, paints an incomplete picture.

Maybe true love isn't off-topic. After all, a house is where one lives, and *where* one lives affects *how* one lives, doesn't it? Maybe even how one loves. Looking around this house, this little, makeshift contraption of a home on wheels that we have been building together for ten years, I am showered in the innumerable memories that Chloe and I have made here (wherever here has been, as we have moved the tiny house several times). Each little invention is connected to a memory, a recollection not only of the things our hands have worked into existence, but of the times during which we worked them—and to be sure, not all of those times were easy to enjoy.

When Chloe and I first imagined a fun fantasy image to introduce this chapter, which is the gateway to our upstairs, we instantly thought of Belle upon the library ladder in *Beauty and the Beast*. It seemed like the perfect picture to tell, not a different truth but a little more of the same truth, which is that we built this house like we built our relationship—with a tremendous amount of love, creativity, and willpower, but with incomplete knowledge of how to properly build something to last—and we have been humbly working to renovate both this house, and our relationship, for some time now.

The tale of renovating true love may not be the fairy tale one is accustomed to reading—but it is an honest look at what the words "happily ever after" truly mean. Besides, there are enough tall tales.

OPPOSITE: *We use the library ladder to access treasures adorning the shelves in our loft area.*

We love to bring new life to old things, like ropes and pulleys, which we also use to hoist our chandelier into place. (It must be lowered during travel.)

Gluing the rose medallions to our ceiling. They bring the design to life and call to mind a Fabergé egg.

Our original painted lattice ceiling. We painted the blue background with a flat finish and the lattice in a gold high-gloss finish to make it appear three-dimensional.

The inspiration for our ceiling came from a picture of an extravagantly trimmed one I spied in <u>Architectural Digest</u>, but re-creating it was too time-consuming and cost prohibitive. As a compromise, we painted a lattice design. Eventually Brandon engineered a more affordable version of that dream lattice. Though less demanding than the original ceiling I'd seen in the magazine, it was still a meticulous, time-consuming project. —C

Cutting out the template for our lattice. We layered it over thin plywood sheets, traced the diamonds, and then router-cut the design.

Using a nail and wire to create the lines on the lattice template. The diamonds in the center are larger than those around the perimeter to accentuate the curve of the ceiling.

We used four shades of blue, fading from dark on the edges to light in the center I painted each diamond with a sponge. —C

I used a flower mold and clay to create the rose medallions. I listened to a few great podcasts while making hundreds of them. —C

Attaching the gold lattice sheets to the painted plywood sheets.

Once the medallions were fired in the oven at home, I spraypainted them and then dusted them with fine gold glitter. I finished with a coating of sealer spray to preserve the effect. —C

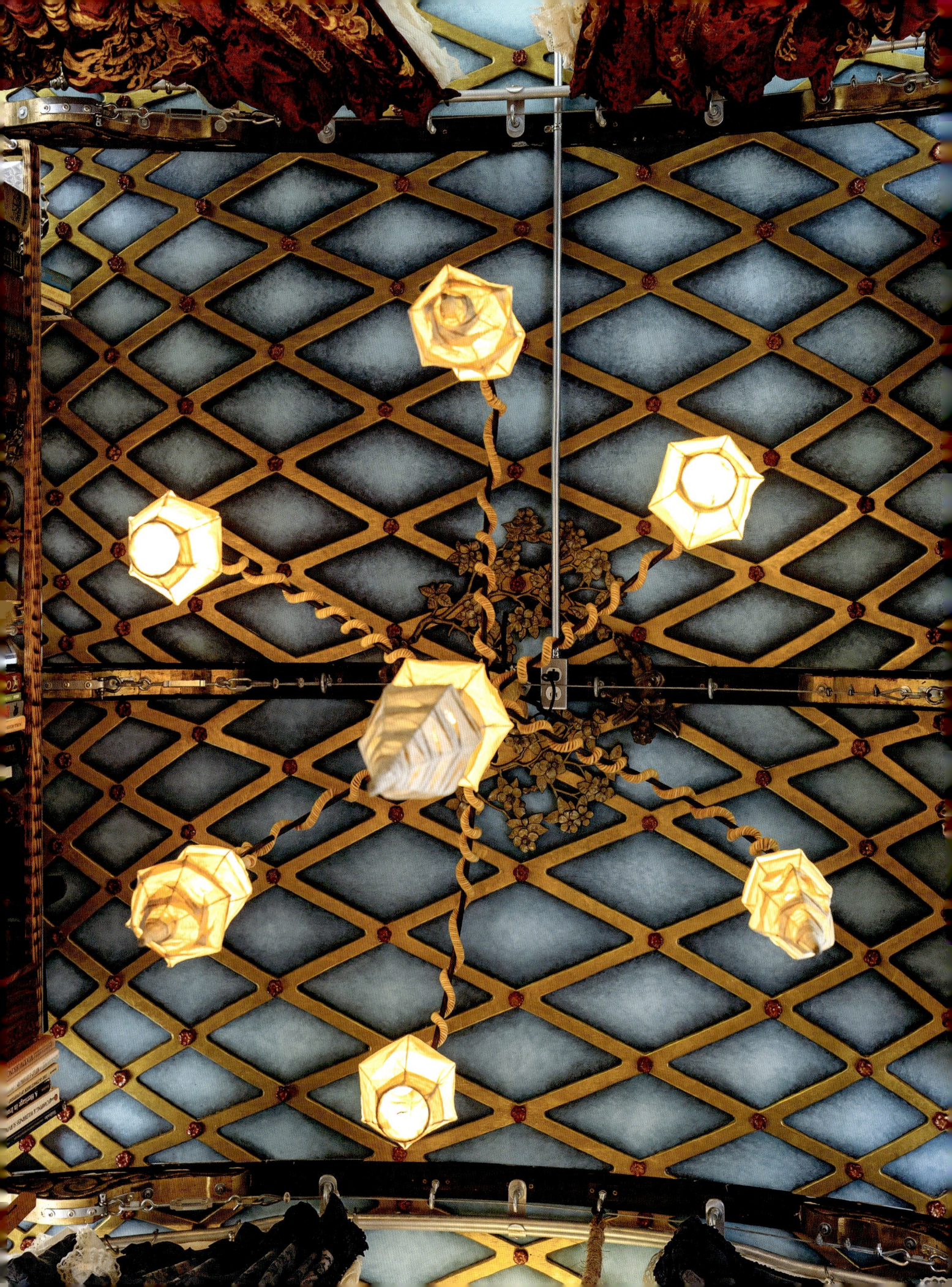

We love to look for ornaments and bits of filigree when we're thrifting. Our favorites are made of brass, but some are plaster, or even plastic. Incorporating them where we can adds luxurious detail for very little investment.

OPPOSITE: *After completing our ceiling, we added filigree, creating a medallion around the chandelier. The adjustable cables that extend across the beams help support the roof.*

Tall Tales

Romantic lighting—whether artificial or natural—has always been a priority in our home. We used acrylic glass sheets for the library shelves so that even though they are arranged over the windows, they don't block the warm glow of afternoon sunlight streaming inside.

Our chandelier fills the space between our lofts; lanterns dangle from its far-reaching octopus arms. We bought the handmade light as set dressing for the first film we worked on, and later purchased it from the director.

These shaved boards were part of a design improvement that added three inches in height to our window walls.

Decorative shelf hangers step the shelf away from the wall to leave room for curtains.

It's hard to believe there was a time when we didn't have storage shelves above our ledges. The walls where the shelves are attached fold down for travel, so the fit must be precise. Using acrylic glass—left over from a set build—makes the space feel more open. A shallow top shelf leaves more of the ceiling visible and gives the illusion that the shelves are taller than they really are. —B

Jazzing up the support pieces with gold-leafing sheets left over from a job.

We also decided to make the shelves transparent so that we can shine light up from underneath at night. Understanding how light can enhance features we wish to highlight has been really useful to us.

The purple insulation behind Chloe's hand shows we hadn't yet added three inches to the other walls.

The ceiling corbels were part of the roof's upgrades. They anchor tension strings that keep the roof bent like a bow. We sanded grooves into and burned the wood for the shelf to make the tiger stripe pattern.

I think I know why antique windows are often so cheap! They need to be completely overhauled, sometimes needing new panes, always needing new glazing putty. To bring our windows back to their original glory, I learned the old-fashioned method of restoration. —C

Glazing the windowpanes with linseed oil-based putty, I got plenty of practice at keeping a steady hand. —C

Using a heat gun is the most efficient way to remove old paint and glazing.

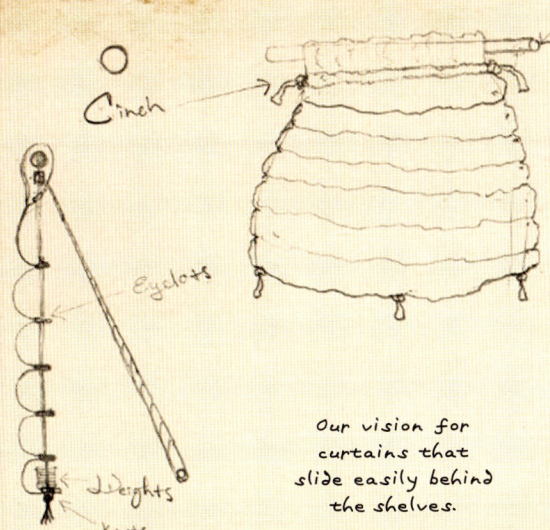

Our vision for curtains that slide easily behind the shelves.

Scraping paint residue off the panes of our newly restored windows.

It is hard to believe that we began building this house ten years ago. We have learned and grown so much wiser since then, and if we were to do it all over again, we would do some things very differently. We are not time travelers, however, so we are forced to cut into the house like a surgeon doing a reconstructive operation. We are students of nature, and when nature shows something doesn't work, we step in and fix it. —B

***In** the span between our bed and the guest sofa, we are afforded room to use creatively. Carving out a little space to display purely decorative pieces feeds our souls.*

LEFT: *The mosaic cake is an art piece I created for fun.* BELOW: *A whimsical ceramic planter with perching doves that my mom found for eight dollars at a church sale.* OPPOSITE: *We enjoy keeping a few succulent plants on the ledge in our loft, where the light is strong. We each have custom-built stowage cabinets that separate the loft space from the office below. They are conveniently covered with meshed metal doors that prevent items from falling out during travel. In my imagination, the ceramic doves flew inside from the windows just beyond.* —C

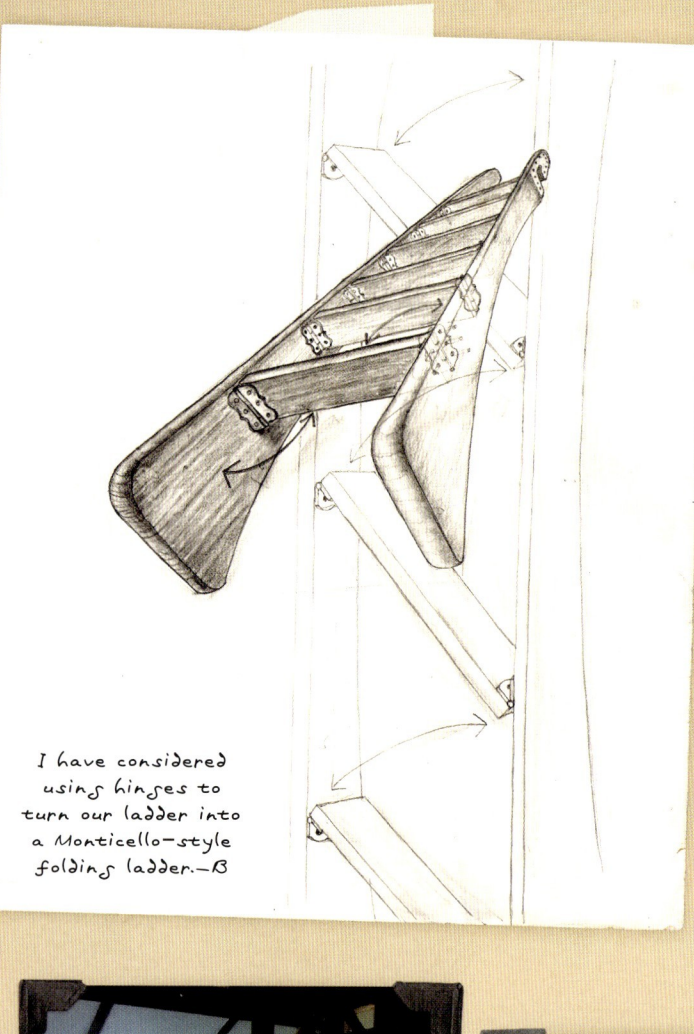

I have considered using hinges to turn our ladder into a Monticello-style folding ladder. —B

Just look at that color! The planks lying on the ground to the left are the same wood—from our original trailer. The hard part was cutting one board in half to make a thinner, lighter ladder out of the heavy wood. —B

I have since added supportive brackets under the rungs to prevent the screws from splitting the wood. —B

There's a little bit of Japanese influence on our design at this phase of construction.

Ten years up and down this ladder—we're like monkeys now. I've only careened headfirst off it once. —B

The black pipe rail makes a useful connection point for the top of the ladder. Designed before we built the shelves above, the ladder currently only connects to the bed and guest sofa. —B

Our loft ladder was inspired by the classic type of library ladder on rails that can be used to zoom whimsically around a room looking for books. We had neither the time nor the money to add wheels when we first built this ladder, though, so alas, there is no zooming. However, now that we have upper shelves to reach, it's time for some upgradings. To start, we'll be extending the black pipe rail around the room. A folding handrail for reaching up high is also in our future.

I found a stationery organizing cabinet at a flea market and trimmed its interior to fit in my overhead compartment.

Judiciously filling these shelves, an ongoing process, has shown us again how details, when not overwhelming, can make a space feel larger.

☙

OPPOSITE: *Threaded rod sheathed in clear rubber tubing ties the shelves together.*
RIGHT: *No curtains yet in this image. We are still fine-tuning the curtain mechanisms.*
BELOW: *I'm obsessed with old books. Thrifting a leatherbound favorite is like Christmas to me.* —B

Dear Diary,

Today, I brought home one of my favorite estate sale finds ever! It's a beautiful crystal basket filled with what I'm sure is the former owner's lifetime collection of assorted decorative strawberries. Some are glass, some are cloth, and others are in a material I don't recognize. There is a special blue-and-gold one, a Victorian pincushion that I now know is worth quite a lot, that I display proudly on top.

This basket came from an estate sale where I found lots of treasures. As I walked around the strawberry lady's home, taking in her many collections and artifacts, I also got a glimpse into her life. It was clear that her collection was curated through adventures and travels, and that each item contained a memory of acquisition. I believe she would have been proud to share those stories had she been there.

Unlike people, objects can't share their origin stories with us, but sometimes, when we hold them in our hands, it's as though we can feel the memories they contain. Even at a young age, I was acutely aware that some items seemed to be sacred. It makes me wonder whether it's possible for the process of creation to imprint energy onto an item, and if so, is it enough energy to affect someone else's life? What might that mean for all of the secondhand finds that surround us? —C

OPPOSITE: I will continue to add any strawberries I come across to the strawberry lady's original collection. The pastel blue Murano glass mirror came from a thrift store. It reflects the color of the ceiling—literally and figuratively. —C

IX

LA VIE EN ROUGE

    Moulin Rouge, the 2001 film starring Nicole Kidman and Ewan McGregor, is the tale of a starry-eyed, lovesick young man who awakens and wins the cynical heart of a showstopping courtesan by boldly singing to her tidbits of various songs. When, at Chloe's invitation, I watched this movie for the first time, I found the opening scenes quite strange, but then the unusual story proved sweet and sad and thought-provoking, and it played out on stages bursting with what I can only describe as a kind of cosmic outpouring of kaleidoscopic light, color, and sound.

    The second time Chloe and I watched this film together, some years later, we noticed that its bold, decorative style had apparently seeped into our own odd little world on wheels, especially our newly renovated sofa/guest-bed/reading getaway. Come to think of it, as I peered over at the new nest, it seemed to embody this aesthetic quite proudly, all the way down to the almost glowing red velvet upholstery beneath the generous helping of colorful throw pillows and mixed blankets. However, as I studied the scene further, I saw that another influence had weaved its way into the tapestry of our subconscious: Dustin Hoffman's pirate ship in *Hook*—another of our favorite films. Its art, too, was clearly present. Indeed, the more I looked, the more influences I noticed, and not just from film, but from everything, everywhere.

    Contemplating this cozy perch of melded inspirations, a familiar question began to form in my mind: How much of what we imagine, how much of what we create, is built of things we have already seen? I confess, I often wonder about creativity. I habitually trip down the rabbit hole of what inspired whom, until I invariably arrive at the safest place to start: the beginning of the universe. Speaking of which, I am reminded of something scientific I recently learned about the beginning of beginnings, and it goes like this. The light of stars that are moving away from us in space stretches, like sound coming from an ambulance that has passed, which shifts the color of the stars' traveling light toward red. This is called "red shift," and it's one of the reasons astrophysicists believe that the universe is expanding, like an explosion, which is how they logically arrive at the Big Bang theory about the beginning of our universe. Unquestionably that was an original creative moment. Some would argue that, like billiard balls after the break, everything seems to have been predictably bouncing around ever since, including our very thoughts.

Now, this big theory is virtually unfathomable and seems designed to perplex and paralyze overthinkers, such as yours truly, to no end. Time and again I have found myself caught in the jaws of this thinking trap, wondering if anyone can truly claim an invention or creation as their own. But something occurred to me one day that has sat well enough with me ever since. Considering the chance, albeit small, that it may help you, dear reader, more easily create, I thought I'd share it: it may be true that every person is born into a world filled with long-existing dreams to draw from, but if we weren't contributing to those dreams, the world would never change. Clearly the world does change, so maybe there are not two competing ways to think about creativity—either we are creative, or we simply pass along a creative baton—but one more complete way to think about it, which is that perhaps that original, creative moment hasn't ended. The beginning of an explosion, after all, is not the whole of one. Even its remotest, most distant ripple is a part of it. Maybe that cosmic spark is alive in everyone and everything, and when we pay very close attention, we can see that red shifting everywhere.

OPPOSITE: *The red fabric on the couch is much brighter than we planned, an unintended consequence of online shopping. In person, it didn't reflect the rich burgundy advertised. Being both frugal and impatient, we decided to embrace our Santa-red couch. It glows brighter than a neon sign when the sun hits, yet still invites us to cozy up with a blanket and a book on a rainy day. We joke that it looks like a pair of giant lips. It's very Dalí.*

This is a sofa made of cushions salvaged from the first sofa we made, which was also made of salvaged cushions. Note Chloe's unfinished office behind.

Our motto is: Do what you can with what you have. Sometimes, we have to break from a project midway through because we lack materials or money, but there always seems to be another project we can jump to in the meantime. —B

This was our first experience with tufting, using fabric that was more forgiving than the faux leather of my chair.

Upholstering hack: Do a lot of stapling.

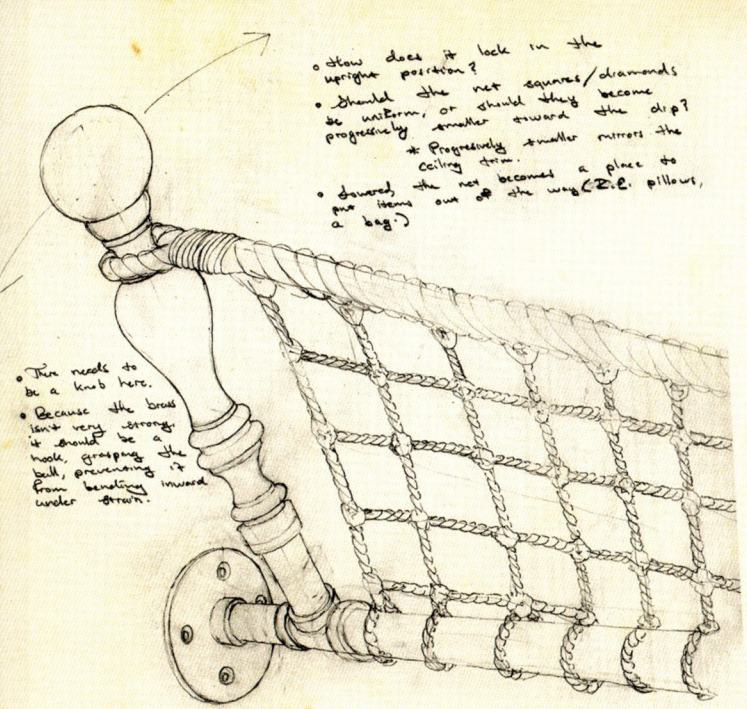

- How does it lock in the upright position?
- Should the net squares/diamonds be uniform, or should they become progressively smaller toward the dip?
  * Progressively smaller mirrors the ceiling form.
- Lowered, the net becomes a place to put items out of the way (i.e. pillows, a bag.)

- There needs to be a knob here.
- Because the brass isn't very strong, it should be a hook, grasping the ball, preventing it from bending inward under strain.

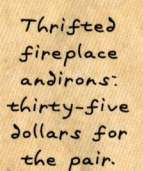

Thrifted fireplace andirons: thirty-five dollars for the pair.

An andiron is reconfigured with black pipe; a threaded rod ties the assemblage together.

Chloe making tufting buttons, one . . . at . . . a . . . time. —B

I confess, I sometimes enjoy doing a tedious task, like making one hundred custom buttons for our couch—an excuse to listen to a good podcast. —C

Weaving a net from natural fiber rope. I actually did this twice. The first net stretched out and got sassy. —B

It is easy to forget that while we were building one thing or another, life was going on: work, stress, challenges. The things we have made embody those memories. Like hieroglyphics in a temple, what surrounds us tells our story. —B

There always seems to be room for one more thing. Finding a place to store blankets was an unanticipated bonus of building our sofa.

The net is designed to prevent guests from plummeting off the sofa while sleeping. It dips in the middle so they can climb over it to get into bed. It hinges forward to a diagonal position and can be filled with decorative pillows that otherwise would be in the way while sleeping. —B

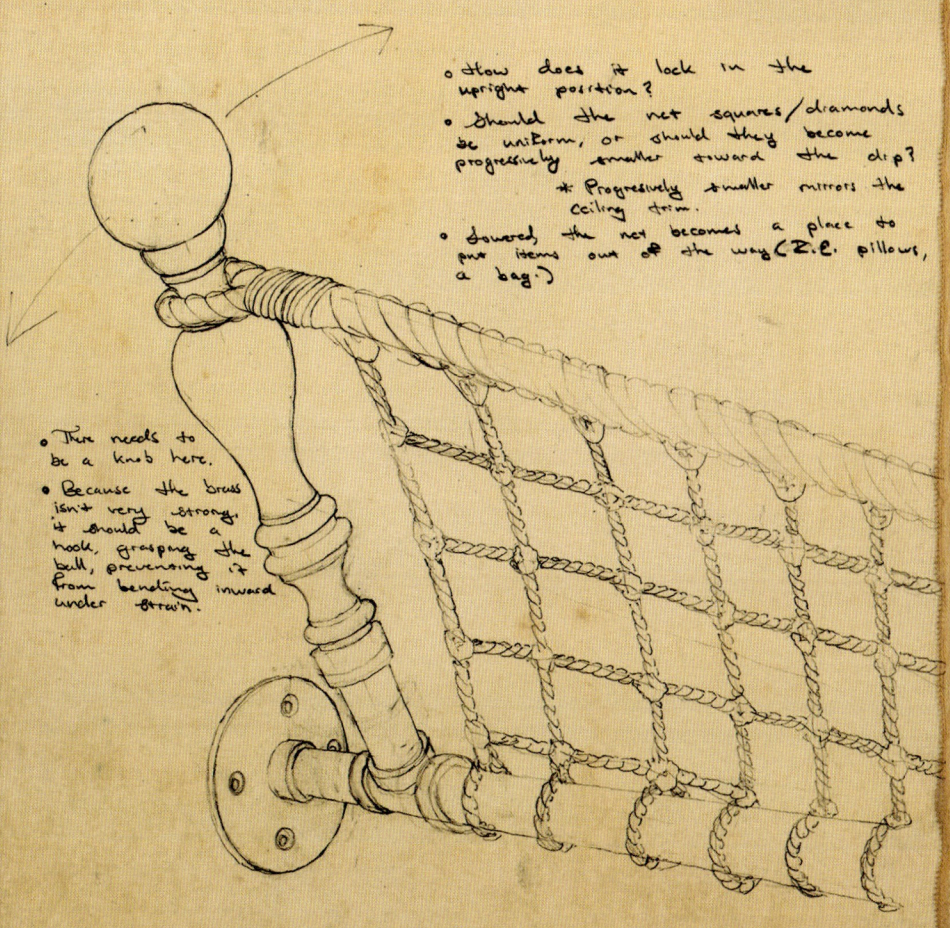

- How does it lock in the upright position?
- Should the net squares/diamonds be uniform, or should they become progressively smaller toward the dip?
  * Progressively smaller mirrors the ceiling form.
- Lowered, the net becomes a place to put items out of the way (i.e. pillows, a bag.)

- There needs to be a knob here.
- Because the brass isn't very strong, it should be a hook, grasping the ball, preventing it from bending inward under strain.

Brandon and I had the idea of hanging curtains in front of the guest sofa. They add privacy and help separate the space. We first found the blue pair, which are actually valances, in the two-dollar bin at a thrift store, and we later added a layer of lace curtains to the backside.

I drew inspiration for the lace curtains from many different sources. I had collected remnants, tablecloths, fabric scraps, and doilies the preceding year. Once I decided which fabrics I wanted to use, I cut the pieces into variously sized rectangles, then pinned together the patchwork curtains. I hired a local seamstress to sew them.

If you are interested in making your own set, I would suggest buying lace fabric that is not too nice to cut up, like synthetic tablecloths from the 1990s, or something else without historical value. I am always conscientious about what I'm upcycling, in service to the artisans who made the pieces. We must preserve important artifacts for future generations, so they can continue to learn the techniques of the past. —C

One of life's pleasures is falling into a soft mound of pillows. —C

OPPOSITE: My mom shared an article with me titled something along the lines of "Decorative Pillows Are Just Stuffed Animals for Grown Women," and I'm not embarrassed to admit it's true. I cultivated this mound by diligently plucking from yard sales and thrift stores. TOP RIGHT: The bold stripes of black-and-white curtains are balanced by these red-striped valances, which are actually part of the curtain set from Brandon's office. Sometimes in design, you can soften the effect by adding to it. BOTTOM RIGHT: A rose pillow I thrifted for two dollars; I later found a matching pink one for five dollars. —C

We love entertaining guests and having a place for them to stay for a sleepover. Our guest sofa is slightly longer than a twin bed, and when topped with its denim featherbed, it becomes a cozy nest for our guests. With the privacy of the curtains, and a bathroom and shower just beneath, it forms a little suite for a hospitable stay. The only conundrum is that there is only one ladder to accommodate both lofts, inevitably leaving someone trapped during the night. —C

The half-chrome light bulb we purchased for our crocheted lamp prevents harsh light from shining downward into our eyes and creates a pleasing ombré glow. At night, the lampshade's crocheted pattern projects onto the ceiling. —B

the SPIRIT of CHRISTMAS

Of all the fine things one might recall from Charles Dickens's *A Christmas Carol*, the memory that most haunts my mind is that of the marvelous draping curtains that cozily ensconce Ebenezer's lonely bed. I can picture them now—those thick, velvet folds, heavily sweeping down around his trembling hands as he peers out, searching the bedroom by the light of a single flickering chamberstick candle. Though Scrooge's draperies were no match for keeping the ghosts at bay, it always seems to me that without them he would have fared worse.

Though my quaintly chilling childhood memory derives, perhaps, less from Dickens's original masterpiece and more from the Mickey Mouse rendition I grew up watching, for as long as I can remember, I always hoped someday to enjoy a bed defended by a sound fortification of fabric. As luck would have it, my own beloved bedfellow's decorative disposition was such that a mere festooning of draperies would be only the beginning of what she intended.

Looking now at the sweep of curtains Chloe has so smartly embellished, I wonder if we haven't come quite close to the mark of my childhood memory, as I cannot help but be spirited back over our years, over all the sweet and challenging moments that have become our own life's story, to the very first time we slept in this bed. The house was brand new and barren and smelled of fresh paint and polyurethane. Without electricity, we lay in the dark, as proud and giddy as children sleeping in a just-finished tree fort for the first time, talking of all the places we would go and of all that might occur.

It is strange to think that we possess the things of which we once only dreamed and that they've become commonplace. It is even easy, if we aren't careful, to take them for granted. And it is stranger still to think that we live now in the future of that early time. From our older and wiser vantage point, our past is golden. It possesses more than we noticed at the time. So, we can only wonder, what might we now have that in the future we may mourn?

It is a sobering thought, and it leaves me with the feeling that I have had my own visits from the ghosts of the past and the future. However, to my fortune, one more spirit remains. But the spirit of Christmas present bears a message that I have found more difficult to grasp than those of the past and future, as enjoying the gift of the present requires not thinking, but being. It's a tricky task to master, but it is practice, they say, that makes perfect. As I lie here, enraptured in a sumptuous candlelit scene of soft linens, the colors of which have somewhere along the line skewed toward a Christmas palette, I find myself sinking deeply into the present, away from future hopes and past regrets. The sensation of enjoying this moment for all that it has to offer is joyfully freeing. Since the present is always upon us, it is a great gift, if only we have the wisdom to live in it.

OPPOSITE: I always feel a deep sense of relief upon crawling into our bed in the evenings. There's something natural and comforting about being removed from the activity below. It must be primal. —C

In a small house, dividing areas without entirely closing them off gives the illusion of more space.

Decorative acorns—thrifted for two dollars—level up a makeshift conduit pipe curtain rod.

Threaded eyebolts provided a useful point of connection to attach custom curtain rod hardware.

This conduit pipe we're using for a curtain rod is meant for running electrical wire. It is cheap and bends handily.

Curtains are a versatile tool for distinguishing spaces. They mark a soft boundary that can be adjusted to one's preference. Open them wide when you're in bed, and the room feels grand. Draw them in tight for cozy seclusion, or part them midway for a little of both.

With the curtains framing above, all we needed was to add a bedframe below.

The curtains were too long, so we folded them in half, pulling the bottoms up and clipping them to the tops.

Our bedframe is one of our favorite free roadside finds. At first we drove by it, but we quickly turned around to give it a closer look. Because it wasn't quite on the curb, we weren't sure if it was actually free.

We don't own a sandblaster or welder (yet), so we farmed those steps out to a local welder.

The daybed came in three pieces—a backboard and two sides. Brandon cut and reconfigured the pieces to fit our loft bed.

After the bed pieces were welded together in their new configuration, we painted them glossy black for gothic flair.

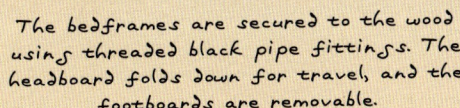

The bedframes are secured to the wood using threaded black pipe fittings. The headboard folds down for travel, and the footboards are removable.

We knocked on the door to double-check, but there was no answer, so we decided to take it and left a note in the mailbox that read, "We took your bed. If that was a mistake, call us." Later we received a voicemail saying the bed had been there for the taking, and the donor hoped we would enjoy it.

OPPOSITE: *Bedside sconces that hinge downward for travel, aglow with (safe) LED candles, make cozy night lighting.* RIGHT: *Our outdoor insulated water barrels provided a reservoir for our water pump to draw from before we had a heated hose. We would fill them with a garden hose—the hose needed to be quickly drained after filling to prevent freezing.*

We've celebrated ten Christmases in our ship-house, some with a bounty of presents, others with few, but we always feel rich in our trove of salvaged trinkets. We keep our eyes open on our travels, and there seem to be presents hiding everywhere.

OPPOSITE: As we get older, it becomes increasingly important to us to mark the passage of time with traditions and celebrations: crafting a gingerbread tiny house, making ornaments by hand, and sharing hot cocoa.
RIGHT: Our loft space feels separate enough to get away when needed, yet still close enough to interact and exchange jokes.

This wreath came from a local thrift haunt's notoriously crowded Christmas sale. Engulfed by frenzied thrifters, I was sure I would leave empty-handed, until I spotted this vintage wreath, glimmering beneath its plain plastic wrapping and sporting an eight-dollar price tag. I knew it was meant for me.—C

There's currently a shortage of Christmas tree real estate in our house, but there's one more present hiding under our floor: a cavern just tall enough to fit a retractable deck someday. It will be the perfect place for our tree.

OPPOSITE: *Brandon reads aloud from* A Tale of Two Cities *while I create an old-fashioned garland from dried orange peels, inspired by the way Victorians used natural elements to handmake decorations.*
CLOCKWISE FROM RIGHT: *Christmas gifts festoon our sofa. Tinseling our tree, reusing as much tinsel as we can; we recently thrifted a set of Victorian wire tinsel for that purpose. We love classic, simple decorations that have stood the test of time.* —C

My dad spotted these curtains. We fell in love but passed, given their hefty price tag. After relentless daydreams, we reconsidered. My mom has a saying Brandon and I like: "Thrift to splurge." That means if you have a habit of saving by thrifting, you can afford to splurge on something once in a while. We are so glad we did. —C

Our bed curtains effortlessly harmonize with our traditional Christmas decorations and make it easy to understand why we chose the spirit of Christmas as this chapter's theme.

We look forward to someday finding that perfect piece of land to park our tiny house for good.

THIS PAGE: *The style of our bedding, an amalgam of thrifted finds, evolved over time. I love to search for rich textiles made from quality fabrics, usually vintage or handmade. Comfort is a priority.* OPPOSITE: *Above the bed, a thrifted shelf has been married to a curtain rod to create a custom valance.*

Parked in a picturesque apple orchard, we weathered our first winter in the tiny house, and we learned a great deal in a short time. We hadn't yet discovered heated hoses, so we tried a variety of odd ways to keep the water running, from blowing out the lines with a compressor to fetching pails of water like Jack and Jill.

Cinched ropes anchor our house and prevent it from trembling in strong winter winds.

There are some things we lament not being able to share more of in the pages of this book, but nothing is so conspicuously lacking as the presence of our entertaining little rabbit Cosmos. Named after the nebulous sprinkling of stars peppering his wolfy coat, he was an integral character in our story, a funny little fable creature who bedazzled our fantasy home. It would have been a treat to spy him in all our photos, but the dear fellow departed for greener pastures almost as soon as we began writing.

I found it especially difficult to adjust to the loss, as Mr. Nose—one of his many aliases—had a habit of perching proudly by my feet whenever I sat down to write. I have missed my little muse. But what would have been a lonelier grieving process was somewhat softened by the community we have come to enjoy where we are currently parked.

When we designed this ship-house, Chloe and I were dreaming of travel, adventure, and self-reliance, but somewhere along our time adrift, we beached in the backyard of Chloe's kin. But what was at first a compromise in our ideal location for the tiny house, over time, we began to see as an opportunity. Relationships grew stronger due to the mutual reliance that living alongside family naturally encourages—something society has drifted away from in the past hundred years or so.

An underrepresented feature of tiny homes is that they can help people to come together, share resources, share space, share company, and share strength. Eventually, we will move again and find ourselves some choice land where we can live out our dreams, but we will depart with a heavy heart. And we will never again go too far away for too long. —B

Christmas in 2017 at the orchard, which also grew Christmas trees. Throwing out a tree at the end of the season is always a little sad, so we asked to borrow one instead. We dug up this Charlie Brown tree, potted it, and returned it to the ground a month later. We also enjoy making walking sticks out of our Christmas trees. —B

∿ EPILOGUE ∿

DOWN *the* LINE

The train is departing, the book is coming to a close, and we're honored you've taken the time to be our guest for a stay. But the journey doesn't end here. This caboose is meant to go somewhere after all. Considering the designs we still have in mind, we haven't yet left the station.

The little green forest hollow of our dreams remains down the line. It's hiding somewhere in New England, waiting to be discovered. There we will carry on building all the little—and not so little—things we weren't able to share with you in this book.

As we wish you a fond farewell, dear reader, we thank you for visiting. And if this book has in some way reached your heart, we would like to express to you how very much we appreciate it. Not every person who has entered our home has found it amusing, which is always what we intended it to be: a gesture of playfulness to embolden any who value living aglow with creativity and spirit. In truth, it is for you we not only wrote this book, but also built this house. We hope that just as a stone cast into the water sends out ripples, the nature of our work will reach you like an encouraging message: you are not alone. However far we are from you in space and time, we tip our hats, nod in recognition, and send you a little warmth of the appreciation we have for the spirit you keep alive.

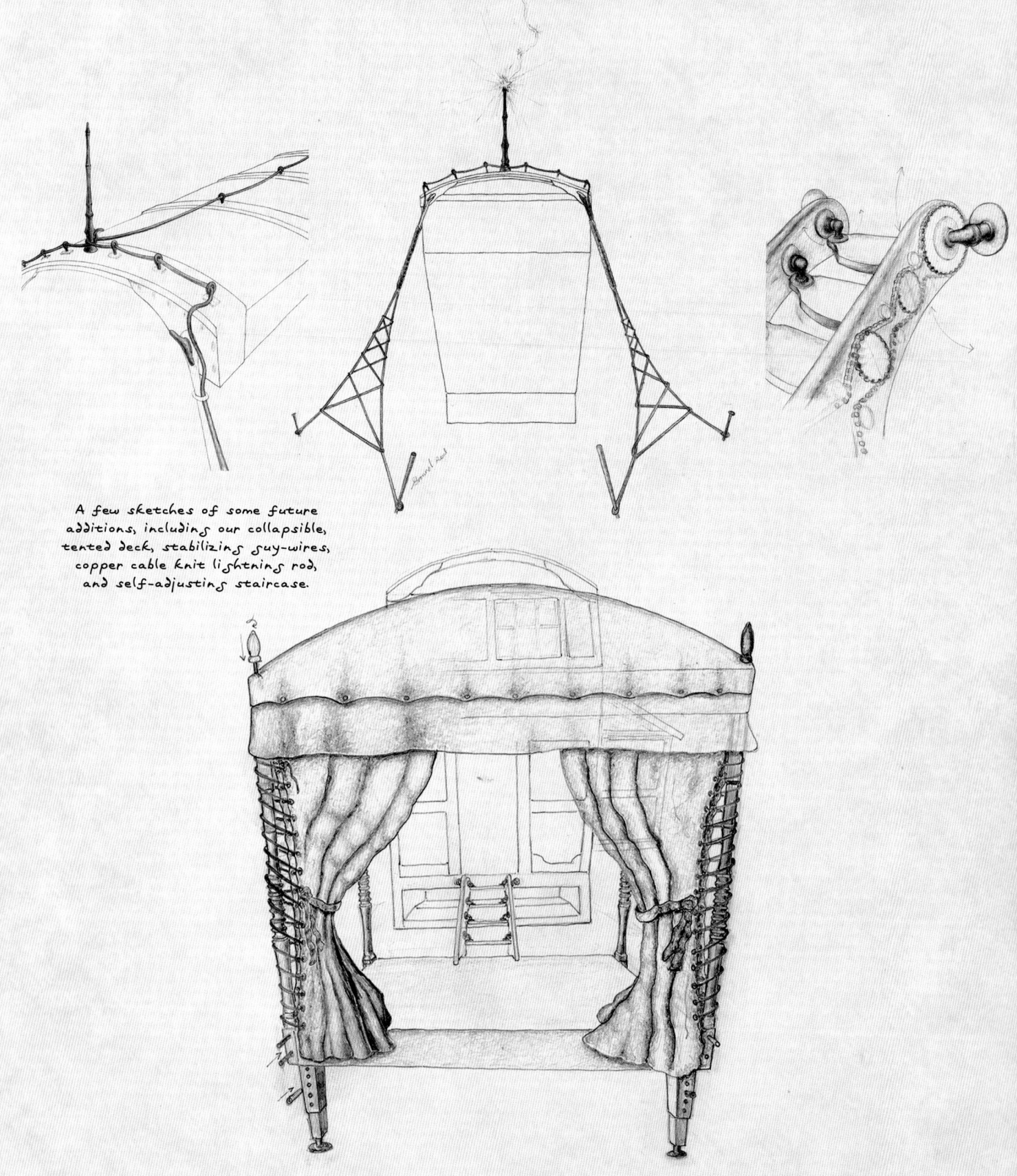

A few sketches of some future additions, including our collapsible, tented deck, stabilizing guy-wires, copper cable knit lightning rod, and self-adjusting staircase.

OPPOSITE: *The view from Saint-Gaudens National Historical Park, overlooking Mt. Ascutney.*

C&B'S LOCAL HAUNTS & FAVORITE SPOTS

Antique Stores

- Deja Vu Furniture & More
  Londonderry, NH
  www.dejavufurniture.net

- Exeter Cam's Antiques
  and My Girlfriend's
  Unique Boutique
  Exeter, NH

- RS Butler's Trading Co.
  Northwood, NH
  www.rsbutlerstradingco.com

- Twice Upon a Time
  Brattleboro, VT
  www.twicetime.com

- Vermont Antique Mall
  Quechee, VT
  www.vermontantiquemall.com

- Windham Antique Center
  Bellows Falls, VT
  www.windhamantiquecentervermont.com

Architectural Salvage

- Architectural Salvage
  Exeter, NH
  www.oldhousesalvage.com

- Nor'east Architectural Antiques
  South Hampton, NH
  www.noreastl.com

- Vermont Salvage
  White River Junction, VT
  www.vermontsalvage.com

Clothing Stores

- April Cornell
  Burlington, VT
  www.aprilcornell.com

- Eileen West
  www.eileenwest.com

- Lanz of Salzburg
  www.lanzofsalzburg.com

- Miss Phyllis
  Manchester Center, VT
  www.missphyllis.net

Film Resources

- Bobby From Boston
  Boston, MA

- 40 South Street
  Jamaica Plain, MA

- Westerman Prop Warehouse
  Worcester, MA

Flea Markets

- Brimfield Flea Market
  Brimfield, MA
  www.brimfieldantiquefleamarket.com

- Elephant's Trunk Flea Market
  New Milford, CT
  www.etflea.com

- The Sturbridge Show
  Sturbridge, MA
  www.thesturbridgeshow.com

- Todd Farm Flea Market
  Rowley, MA
  www.thetoddfarm.com

General Stores and Markets

- Brownsville Butcher & Pantry
  Brownsville, VT
  www.butcherandpantry.com

- Hemingway Farms
  Charlestown, NH
  www.hemingwayfarms.com

- Singletons General Store
  Proctorsville, VT
  www.singletonsvt.com

- Vermont Country Deli
  Brattleboro, VT
  www.vermontcountrydeli.com

- The Vermont Country Store
  Bellows Falls, VT
  www.vermontcountrystore.com

- Walker Farm
  Dummerston, VT
  www.walkerfarm.com

- Walpole Valley Farms
  Walpole, NH
  www.walpolevalleyfarms.com

Picnic Spot

- Saint-Gaudens National
  Historical Park
  Cornish, NH
  www.nps.gov/saga/index.htm

Specialty Shops

- Boston General Store
  Brookline, MA
  www.bostongeneralstore.com

- The Chester Bookworm
  Chester, VT
  www.chesterbookworm.com

- L.A. Burdick
  Walpole, NH
  www.burdickchocolate.com

- Penelope Wurr
  Brattleboro, VT
  www.penelopewurr.com

- Pickwick's Mercantile
  Portsmouth, NH
  www.pickwicksmercantile.com

- Seed to Stem
  Worcester, MA
  www.shopseedtostem.com

- Tailor Bird Sewing
  Claremont, NH
  www.tailorbirdsewing.com

Thrift Stores

- The Blessing Barn
  Mendon, MA
  www.theblessingbarn.com

- Boomerang
  Brattleboro, VT
  www.boomerangvermont.com

- Camille's Experienced
  Clothing
  Rutland, VT
  www.camillesvt.com

- Cover Home Repair
  White River Junction, VT
  www.coverhomerepair.org

- Experienced Goods
  Brattleboro, VT
  www.expgoods.com

- Listen Thrift Stores
  White River Junction, VT;
  Lebanon, NH; Canaan, NH
  www.listencs.org/thrift-stores

- M&C
  Amherst, NH
  www.mcclothingandgifts.com

- The Renaissance Shoppe
  New London, NH
  www.lakesunapeevna.org

Keywords for Searches

1950s, 1970s, Baroque, Brass, Chic, Classic, Copper, Cottage, Cottagecore, Country, Eccentric Furniture, Eclectic, Embroidered, Floral, Folk, French, French Country, Gilded, Gold, Gothic, Handcrafted, Handmade, Hand-painted, Neoclassical, Old, Patchwork, Patina, Prairie, Rare, Reclaimed, Retro, Rococo, Ruffled, Salvaged, Silver, Steampunk, Toile, Tudor, Victorian/Edwardian, Vintage

A Few of Chloe's Favorite Brand Name Searches

Anthropologie, Ethan Allen, Free People, Gunne Sax, House of Hackney, Jessica McClintock, Laura Ashley, Magnolia Pearl, Nathalie Lété, Pendleton, Pottery Barn, Rachel Ashwell, Ralph Lauren, Restoration Hardware, Tasha Tudor, Waverly, William Morris, Williams-Sonoma

ACKNOWLEDGMENTS

The lovely people you see on these pages are the friends and family who helped bring our house to life, along with the team who became friends and family while making this book. We are so profoundly grateful to all of you, including those not pictured here—Jason Abramowicz, Jacob Brown, Joel Robison, Hooroo Jackson, and Scott Minchin—for the belief, support, and encouragement you have gifted us. Some of you brought tools to help build, some brought ideas, and others brought resources, but all of you brought hope. Without you, our dream would still be just a dream. We will never forget you. If you ever need a place to stay, there's a little room on our couch.

Valarie Michaud and John Hession

Mary Randolph Carter

Hally Sheely

Lynn and Gerhard Blume

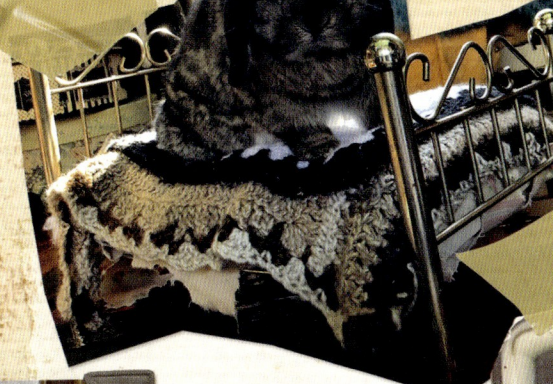

Cosmos AKA Mr. Nose

The Steiners

Kathy and Steve Paine

First published in the United States of America in 2025 by
Rizzoli International Publications, Inc.
49 West 27th Street
New York, NY 10001
www.rizzoliusa.com

Copyright © 2025 Chloe Barcelou and Brandon Batchelder
Foreword: Mary Randolph Carter

All rights reserved. No part of this publication
may be reproduced, stored in a retrieval system, or
transmitted in any form or by any means, electronic,
mechanical, photocopying, recording, or otherwise,
without prior consent of the publishers.

Publisher: Charles Miers
Senior Editor: Kathleen Jayes
Design: Celia Fuller
Production Manager: Barbara Sadick
Managing Editor: Lynn Scrabis

ISBN: 978-0-8478-3428-0
Library of Congress Control Number: 2024945543

PRINTED IN HONG KONG

2025 2026 2027 2028 / 10 9 8 7 6 5 4 3 2 1

Visit us online:
Instagram.com/RizzoliBooks
Facebook.com/RizzoliNewYork
X: @Rizzoli_Books
Youtube.com/user/RizzoliNY

PHOTOGRAPHY CREDITS

Jennifer Bakos: Endpapers, pages 7, 8, 9, 11, 32, 33, 43, 44, 48, 51, 66, 67, 74, 75, 80, 81, 87, 89, 90, 91, 92, 93, 95 (top left), 96, 97, 99, 104, 105, 109, 110 (top left), 111, 118 (top left), 120, 121, 123, 128, 129, 132, 133, 134, 135, 136, 137, 138, 139, 140, 144, 145, 151, 156, 157, 161, 162, 164, 165, 166, 167, 168, 170, 171, 172, 173, 177, 178, 179, 184, 186–87, 188, 189, 192, 193, 195, 196–97, 198, 201, 205, 209 (bottom left and right), 210, 214–15, 216, 217, 218, 219, 223, 224, 225, 230, 231, 232–33, 234, 235, 236–37, 238, 241, 251
Olivia Barcelou: Pages: 224, 225
Hannah DuBois: Page 39
John W. Hession: Pages: 29, 36, 86, 185, 252
Morgan Karanasios: Pages: 4, 49, 59, 64–65, 68–69, 70–71, 72–73, 79, 84, 85, 88, 103, 108, 113, 114, 115, 119, 127, 141, 142–43, 146, 147, 148–49, 155, 160, 163, 169, 180–81, 199, 212–13, 224, 228, 240, 242–43, 247
Joel Robison: Pages: 14, 26, 56, 76, 100, 124, 152, 156 (top left postcard) 174, 202, 220, 239, 248
3Sixty Photography: Pages: 20, 21
Cover: Morgan Karanasios, Joel Robison, and John W. Hession
All other images courtesy of the authors.